D0908262

LAKELAND'S GREATEST PIONEERS

Lakeland's Greatest Pioneers

A Hundred Years of Rock Climbing

by

Bill Birkett

ROBERT HALE · LONDON

© *T. W. Birkett 1983*
First published in Great Britain 1983

ISBN 0 7090 0537 7

Robert Hale Limited
Clerkenwell House
Clerkenwell Green
London EC1R 0HT

Photoset by
Kelly Typesetting Limited
Bradford-on-Avon, Wiltshire
Printed in Great Britain by
Redwood Burn Limited
Trowbridge, Wiltshire
Bound by W.B.C. Bookbinders Limited

Contents

To Ruth, wife and mother of two Lakeland Pioneers

Illustrations

PICTURE CREDITS

Reproduction of illustrations has been permitted by the following:
Su Harvey, map and sketches on pp. 15, 17, 19, 21 and 25; Jim
Birkett, 1, 3, 21, 24, 31; Marie Blake, 30; Sid Cross, 13, 14, 15, 18,
19; Fell and Rock Climbing Club, 4, 5, 6, 7, 11, 12; Dennis Grey,
29; H. J. Jenkins, 2, 8, 9, 16, 17, 20, 28; Dave Kay, 23; P. Livesey,
34; Bill Peascod, 25, 26, 27; I. Roper, 22, 32, 33, 35; Yorkshire
Rambling Club, 10.

Erratum　The caption to the ninth picture in the second section
(no. 26) should read as above.

Drawings in the Text

The following four sketches illustrate the progressive development of climbing style and equipment:

Acknowledgements

So many people have gone out of their way to help me, and it is they who have made this project possible. Please forgive me for not listing everybody but I am indebted to A. Austin, Austin-Barton, B. Beck, J. Birkett, M. Blake, J. Bloor, J. Brown, D. Cook, J. Cook, A. Craven, S. and J. Cross, E. Downham, H. Drasdo, J. Farrington, M. Files, D. Grey, P. Harding, A. Hargreaves, P. Livesey, R. Matheson, B. Peascod, Su Harvey for the artwork, Bert Jenkins and Ian Roper for their photography and Pat Forsyth and Barbara Miller for the typing.

I would also like to express my appreciation to the following for permission to quote copyright material: Fell and Rock Climbing Club, 33, 35, 36, 73, 74, 75, 76, 81, 83, 84, 88, 91, 97, 102, 118, 123, 161; E. J. Wilson, 43, 46, 49, 51, 53, 63; Yorkshire Ramblers' Club, 64; Victor Gollancz Ltd., 109; the Society of Authors at the literary representative of the Estate of A. E. Housman, and Jonathan Cape Ltd., publishers of A. E. Housman's *Collected Poems*, 148; Pete Livesey, 177.

Introduction

This book tells the story of Lakeland rock-climbing development, the achievements, the excitement and the tragedies, not as a definitive history but as it was shaped by the lives and climbs of its greatest pioneers. These men, who have been at the forefront of rock-climbing development, are extreme and consequently fascinating personalities. For each individual I have not only examined their climbing record but also portrayed their life style and personality. The resulting story is not only one which will intrigue, and surprise, those interested in rock climbing and mountaineering but also one which will appeal to the many fascinated by English history.

The English Lake District was the birthplace of a new phenomenon now known as rock climbing. I say 'phenomenon' for rock climbing is more than a sport: it is a way of life for many and, unfortunately, for the few a way of death. Its reason lies solely within the individual and, unlike Alpinism and mountaineering, it is the immediate difficulty or quality of surmounting or finding a unique way up a particular piece of rock that counts, not the goal of reaching the summit. Rock climbers are born not created. It is in the blood, for this outwardly pointless activity requires considerable physical and mental strength, dedication and just the right balance of courage and commitment.

Although the Lakeland Fells are small in comparison with the mountain ranges of the world, their activists in their philosophies and techniques, have had a profound effect on world climbing and mountaineering. As it was the birthplace of rock climbing, the Lake District has mirrored and often led the standards of difficulty. The pioneers selected for this book have all significantly raised the threshold of what was imagined possible by their predecessors.

Rock climbing began as a distinct and separate entity in the 1880s with W. P. Haskett-Smith. During the intervening hundred years there have been very many, occasionally brilliant, climbers. I have been rather brutal and selected only eleven individuals; consequently the climbers chosen are truly Lakeland's greatest pioneers. They are listed in chronological order of performance:

W. P. Haskett-Smith
O. G. Jones
F. Botterill
S. Herford
H. M. Kelly
A. T. Hargreaves
R. J. Birkett
W. Peascod
A. Dolphin
A. Austin
P. Livesey

I love the mountains, particularly the Lakeland fells, and have lived and worked amongst them all my life. To me Lakeland climbs are like jewels. Their boldness, length and elegance of line may be equalled, perhaps bettered, but the intricacies and technicalities contained within their tiny frame are unsurpassable.

Perhaps because my father is one of the greatest rock climbers, I have always found the people and the characters of the mountains almost as interesting as the hills themselves. For pioneering new climbs is as much about personality as it is pure physical action. In writing and researching this book I have been fortunate in meeting many people who love the fells as I do, and it has been a great joy for me merely to talk about and reminisce over our precious days on the hills.

1

A Brief History of Climbing and Equipment Development

Rock climbing is now a hundred years old, and from its glorious beginnings to the present day there have been many significant waves of development. It began in the Lake District, when one man decided that the actual thrill of climbing superseded that of reaching the summit, that tackling the most difficult way up a crag rather than the easiest, and pitting one's physical and mental powers against a problem and beating it were indeed pleasurable! Walter Parry Haskett-Smith was the first true rock-climbing pioneer, and the year was 1881. Many great men were to follow his initiative, and from this simple beginning climbing techniques, equipment and standards have developed beyond even his most ambitious expectations.

Due to the advent of better communications, principally the Furness Railway serving Cumberland's west coast, tourism became a booming industry. It became a relatively simple matter for the Victorian 'elite' to visit the Lake District. Consequently the tiny hamlet of Wasdale Head, its guest houses and hotel, became the focal point for all aspiring rock climbers. Imagine it as it was then, nestling below England's highest mountain, Scafell Pike, and the mighty Great Gable, isolated yet accessible, enticing yet virgin.

The years that followed Haskett-Smith's lead were magnificent. Here intelligent and serious-minded Victorian gentlemen, oppressed by the great industrial age and family ritual, were set free. Scientists, doctors, engineers and teachers all came to the Wasdale Head to sample the new sport and 'let their hair down'.

The resultant wave of rock-climbing popularity and development was inspired. This era from the 1880s until the early 1900s became known as the 'Golden Age' of rock climbing.

Techniques were primitive, and the entire safety of a climbing team lay with the leading climber. If the leader fell off, then the consequences for the entire party were grave. The climbers in general simply tied themselves together, with heavy, unreliable hemp rope, and set off, albeit spaced out, up a rock face. Often they would climb together in this fashion. On their feet they wore heavy and clumsy leather boots, some with nails, some without, and it was often the fashion to carry a long ice-axe for 'assistance'.

Into this scene came a brilliant, energetic and forceful man, an honours graduate in experimental physics, who was determined to climb harder and yet harder. He shattered the climbing scene, producing routes that were previously thought impossible. The man, O. G. Jones, sears the imagination, for he produced routes that remain at a very severe standard even today. He invented the first system of classifying routes in order of difficulty and also devised more scientific methods of rope handling—inventing the running belay. (A belay secures the climber to the rock face as opposed merely to his companions.)

He graded routes as follows: Easy, Moderate, Difficult and Exceptionally Severe. Today much the same system is used, as follows: Easy—a scramble; Moderate (M)—more of a climb; Difficult (D)—can only be climbed; Very Difficult (VD): Mild Severe (MS); Severe (S); Hard Severe (HS); Mild Very Severe (MVS); Very Severe (VS); Hard Very Severe (HVS); Extremely Severe (E1 to E5). These gradings take into account both the seriousness and the technical difficulty of the climb. Because these days very hard climbs can be protected with modern techniques ('nut runners' used as running belays), a climb can be

1890s: Early days—clumsy boots and "the Only Genuine Jones"

technically very hard, yet if a leader falls, then the chances of injury are considerably minimized. So an additional system of purely grading technical difficulty has been devised; this includes a number suffixed by the letters a, b or c. 1a would be a Difficult (D) climb; 1b a harder Difficult (D) climb; 1c an even harder Difficult climb. Generally the technical grade is used only for the harder routes, Very Severe or above. i.e., VS climbs have technical difficulty of 4a, 4b or 4c, and a Hard VS could be 4c or even 5a. In Lakeland the hardest technical difficulty so far achieved has been 6b. The hardest Lakeland climbs are now graded E5 6b.

After the 'easy-way-up' period came Haskett-Smith, whose most remarkable climb was undoubtedly his solo ascent of Napes Needle (D) in 1886. Then along came Jones, whose most notable routes were C Gully (MVS) in 1897, Kern Knotts Crack (MVS) in 1897 and Walker's Gully (HS) in 1899. It should be noted that in the space of eleven years the standard of climbing was raised five full grades of difficulty by Jones.

Most new routes put up in this era before the twentieth century were climbed in the gullies and chimneys that split the main buttresses of rock. Understandably these early climbers felt more secure in such obvious features, shielded to a certain extent by the confining walls. In actual fact, many of these early gully climbs were harder if less serious than the climbs up the open walls that were to follow. This period in climbing history 1881 to the mid 1890s is known as the 'Gully and Chimney' period.

It was Jones who took the initiative and daringly, almost suicidally, blasted his way up the great open face of the four-hundred-foot Scafell Pinnacle in 1896. Such was the magnitude of this climb that it was sixteen years before it was repeated. It was also the scene of a tragic accident in 1903, when a party of four climbers fell whilst attempting the second ascent and were all killed. Jones's ascent marked the possibility of the 'Slab and Wall' era.

But before others were able to follow his initiative there was another type of climbing that should be mentioned. This was the 'Ridge and Arete' period, where ordinary mortals, unlike Jones, dared to leave the gullies but not yet tackle the open and apparently blank faces and slabs of rock. Instead, ridges and the obviously sharply defined edges of the buttresses (aretes) were tackled. Most outstanding of these was undoubtedly G. A. Solly's

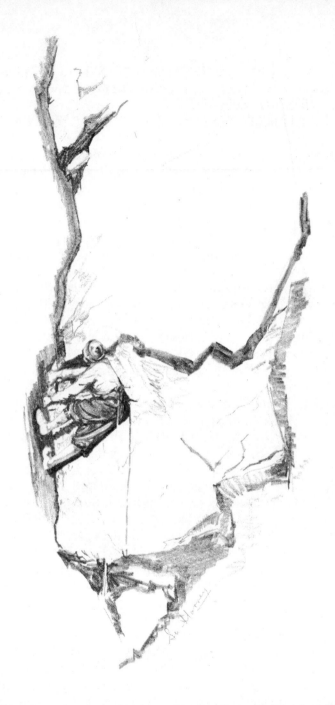

1920s: Introduction of 'rubbers' and science by H. M. Kelly

ascent of Eagle's Nest Ridge Direct (MVS) in 1892. This route remains an unprotected and serious lead to this day and has seen many falls and fatalities.

Fred Botterill's ascent of Botterill's Slab (VS) in 1903 was ahead of its time, and it was not until S. W. Herford and G. S. Sansom arrived in 1912 that Jones's route on Scafell and Botterill's Slab received second ascents. The later two climbers spearheaded what promised to be a new and great generation of climbers. Ropes and rope-handling techniques were now considerably better than before; footwear had improved, if but slightly, with a better system of nails approved and popularized by the famous Abraham brothers. Boots, however, remained heavy, clumsy and eminently unsuitable for the delicate footwork required on this new generation of climbs. Indeed, climbers often removed their boots, recognizing their danger, and climbed in socks or bare feet. In 1914, riding the crest of a wave, they climbed the great Central Buttress on Scafell (HVS), a milestone in climbing history. It was a doomed generation. By the end of the 1914–18 war a whole generation of climbers had been destroyed.

Surprisingly, by the 1920s climbing was more popular and, if possible, more inspired than before. The leader of this new era was H. M. Kelly, who put up many very severe climbs and two of Lakeland's classics, Tophet Wall (S) in 1923 and Moss Ghyll Grooves (MVS) in 1926. Even more significant was his modern outlook on climbing and its consequent effect for others. He took a searching look at equipment and introduced a new, superior form of footwear—'rubbers'. He also improved safety techniques with sophisticated belays and rope management. Probably his greatest contribution was that of the modern guidebook, enabling and encouraging many more people to climb. He climbed and pioneered systematically, setting an example for others to follow.

In the early thirties the pace of exploration slowed considerably, and it was A. T. Hargreaves who opened the decade with the tough Deer Bield Cracks (HVS 5a). The end of the 1930s was rocked by an unknown local lad and his ascent in 1938 of May Day Climb (HVS 5c) and East Buttress Girdle (HVS 5a) on Scafell. Jim Birkett was the first of the 'common men' to enter a 'gentleman's sport'. He was a natural climber, Britain's finest, and he dominated climbing for over a decade. His routes, whatever their grade, are all of high quality, and he took nailed-boot

1940s: The ultimate use of 'nails' by Jim Birkett

climbing to a frightening degree, climbing the hardest routes of
his day in 'waisted clinkers', 'tricounis' and even quarryman's
clogs. Producing Britain's first Extreme, Harlot Face (E1), his
protection techniques were primitive by any standards, for he
used only hemp slings as running belays and placed them
sparingly. His ascent of Overhanging Bastion (VS) on Castle
Rock in 1939 was a breakthrough in concept.

Bill Peascod climbed throughout the 1940s and extensively
developed the north-western Fells. He is noted for his long,
unprotected leads at a high technical level. Significantly he is
responsible not only for over fifty new climbs but for discovering,
and popularizing, a number of major crags, particularly in the
Buttermere Valley. These include Eagle Front (VS) on Eagle
Crag—Buttermere, Dexter Wall (VS) on Grey Crag—Buttermere, Cleopatra (HVS) on Buckstone Howe, and Falconers
Crack (VS) on Eagle Crag—Borrowdale.

Arthur Dolphin, particularly with his ascent of Kipling Groove
(HVS) in 1948, heralded a new generation of climbers which
arrived in the 1950s. He went on to put up some remarkable
Extreme climbs, notably Deer Bield Buttress (E1) in 1951 and
Hell's Groove (E1) in 1952. Although his protection techniques
and equipment were better than Birkett's and Peascod's, he was
still using only slings for running belays, pitons being very strictly
against his code of ethics. He did, however, have nylon ropes
which were much more reliable, lighter and consequently easier
to handle than the old 'Alpine line'.

During the 1950s transport became much easier to obtain,
usually in the form of the motorbike, and climbing was now a
pastime actively indulged in by all social classes. From the late
fifties up to the present day, it becomes an extremely difficult task
to single out particular pioneers, because there have been many
very fine climbers. From the mid 1950s to the 1970s Alan Austin
was probably the single most influential and prolific Lakeland
pioneer. Not only did he put up some hard and beautiful climbs
but, perhaps more importantly, he fought an ethical war against
the indiscriminate use of the piton, and won.

During this period the advance in climbing equipment was
phenomenal. Footwear was improved a hundred per cent by the
widespread use of the vibram rubber-soled boot and the PAs, a
tight-fitting, high-friction 'baseball-type' shoe imported from

1980s: Headband and chalk, the modern rock athlete
inspired by Pete Livesey

France. Protection techniques were thought out and radically altered. The introduction of the 'nut runner' made climbing much safer, in fact a quite different game from that played prior to the 1960s.

Austin's finest routes are most probably Astra (E1), 1960, Razor Crack (E1 5a), 1966, Chimney Variant (E2 5b), 1966, and Brackenclock (E2 5b), 1970. Yet by the 1970s, although the equipment had advanced out of all recognition from that used by Birkett and Dolphin, the standard of climbing, although undoubtedly harder, had not risen proportionally.

A number of isolated routes stand out as being harder than the rest. The Vikings (Richard McHardy—E3 6a), 1969, Lord of the Rings (J. Adams and Colin Read, E2 5c), 1969, Paladin (Rob Matheson, E3 5c), 1970, Brain Damage (Ed Grindly, E3 6a), 1973 and Pearl's Before Swine (P. Long, E3 5c), 1973. But then in 1974 the climbing world was shocked from relative complacency by an explosion of frighteningly hard routes climbed by Pete Livesey.

These routes were something really special, two full grades harder than any other pioneer in Britain had achieved. Livesey showed what was possible with dedication, training and the application of modern protection techniques. He realized that it was now possible to make desperate moves safely, that one could perform on a boulder a few feet off the ground, high on a cliff face. In fact, the climber could rely on his nut protection to prevent 'injury' if a fall occurred, providing his nuts stayed in place! With this attitude of total commitment, he achieved the largest single step in climbing standards for twenty years. His routes were not only very hard but, more importantly, very good. Particularly notable are Footless Crow (E5 6b), 1974, Bitter Oasis (E3 6a), 1974 and Lost Horizons (E4 6a), 1976.

Today Lakeland climbing is in a very healthy state. There are a number of pioneers putting up routes of a standard comparable to Livesey's 1970s creations and many more climbers who climb these existing routes in good style. While the crags wait silently for the next great pioneer, we, the climbers, can enjoy the products of a hundred years of exploration, ranging from Easy to Extremely Severe (E5 6b), from Haskett-Smith to Pete Livesey. Above everything else, we can climb for the best reason of all—for the fun of it.

LAKELAND'S GREAT ROUTES

The following is a list of the most significant and historically important routes, numbered and shown on the sketch plan, and also the routes giving the very best climbing achieved by the eleven pioneers chosen in this book.

No.		Route Name	Grade	Location	Pioneer's Name	Climbers' Comment
	1882	Great Gully	Difficult (D)	Pavey Ark, Langdale	W. P. Haskett-Smith	One of the first great gully climbs.
1)	1884	Needle Ridge	Difficult (D)	Napes, Great Gable	W. P. Haskett-Smith	
	1886	Napes Needle	Difficult (D)	Napes, Great Gable	W. P. Haskett-Smith	The most famous climb and still not easy.
2)	1896	Jones's Route from Deep Ghyll	Severe (S)	Scafell Pinnacle	O. G. Jones	A very daring lead up an exposed face of rock.
	1897	C Gully	Mild Very Severe (MVS)	Wasdale Screes	O. G. Jones	In the then traditional gully mode—but harder!
3)	1897	Kern Knotts Crack	Mild Very Severe (MVS)	Kern Knotts, Great Gable	O. G. Jones	A new concept in climbing following a vertical crack in a smooth wall.
	1898	Jones's Route	Hard Very Difficult (HVD)	Dow Crag	O. G. Jones	A curving corner crack climbed on his way to Wasdale.
4)	1899	Walker's Gully	Mild Very Severe (MVS)	Pillar Rock	O.G. Jones	An epic climbed in the ice with stockinged feet!
	1903	Botterill's Slab	Very Severe (VS)	Scafell	F. W. Botterill	Beautiful, bold, technical climb ten years ahead.
	1906	North West Climb	Mild Very Severe (MVS)	Pillar Rock	F. W. Botterill	Long and difficult.
	1907	Crescent Climb	Moderate	Pavey Ark	F. W. Botterill	Magnificently easy.
	1909	Abbey Buttress	Very Difficult			
	1912	Kern Knotts West Buttress	Mild Very Severe	Kern Knotts, Great Gable	G. S. Sansom and S. Herford	Steep and interesting, a taste of things to come.

No.		Route Name	Grade	Location	Pioneer's Name	Climbers' Comment
5)	1914	Central Buttress	Hard Very Severe (HVS)	Scafell	S. W. Herford	A great leap forward in difficulty and impressiveness.
	1919	Sodom & Gomorrah Routes 1 & 2	Very Severe (VS)	Pillar Rock	H. M. Kelly	Modern in concept
	1922	Kern Knotts West Buttress	Hard Very Severe (HVS)	Kern Knotts	H. M. Kelly	Vintage Kelly.
	1922	Flake Climb	Very Severe (VS)	Kern Knotts	H. M. Kelly	Excellent climbing.
	1923	The Appian Way	Hard Severe (HS)	Pillar Rock	H. M. Kelly	One of the best climbs of its grade.
	1923	Tophet Wall	Hard Severe (HS)	Tophet Buttress Great Gable	H. M. Kelly	Superb.
6)	1926	Moss Ghyll Grooves	Hard Severe (HS)	Scafell	H. M. Kelly	An obvious natural line.
	1928	Grooved Wall	Very Severe (VS)	Pillar Rock	H. M. Kelly	Hard and even today devoid of protection.
7)	1930	Deer Bield Crack	Hard Very Severe (HVS)	Deer Bield, Easedale	A. T. Hargreaves	Delightful.
		Direct Route	Mild Very Severe (MVS)	Castle Rock, South Crag	A. T. Hargreaves	
	1932	Nor'nor'West Climb	Very Severe (VS)	Pillar Rock	A. T. Hargreaves	
	1933	Overhanging Wall	Very Severe	East Buttress, Scafell	A. T. Hargreaves and M. Linnel (lead)	Well named.
8)	1938	May Day Climb	Hard Very Severe (HVS)	East Buttress, Scafell	R. J. Birkett	Technically very hard.
		East Buttress Girdle	Hard Very Severe (HVS)	East Buttress, Scafell	R. J. Birkett	A recognized challenge.
9)	1939	Overhanging Bastion	HVS	Castle Rock	R. J. Birkett	Massive psychological breakthrough showing possibilities.
	1940	North West Arete	MVS	Gimmer Crag	R. J. Birkett	Good.
		F Route	VS	Gimmer Crag	R. J. Birkett	Fine Line.

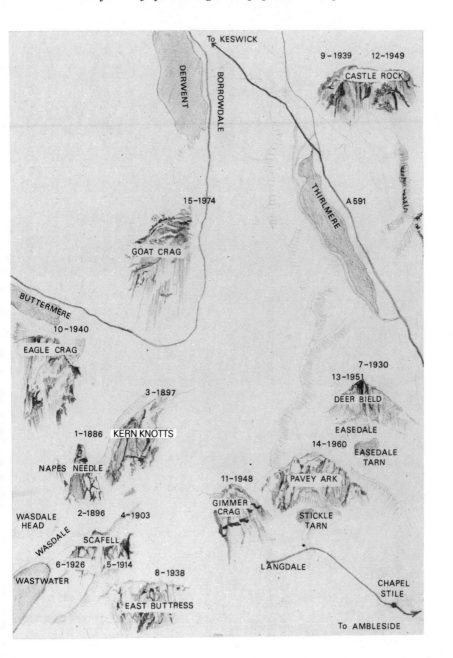

To KESWICK

9 – 1939   12 – 1949

CASTLE ROCK

DERWENT

BORROWDALE

THIRLMERE

A 591

15 – 1974

GOAT CRAG

BUTTERMERE

10 – 1940

EAGLE CRAG

7 – 1930

13 – 1951

DEER BIELD

3 – 1897

EASEDALE

1 – 1886   KERN KNOTTS

14 – 1960

EASEDALE TARN

NAPES NEEDLE

11 – 1948

PAVEY ARK

GIMMER CRAG

WASDALE HEAD

2 – 1896   4 – 1903

STICKLE TARN

WASDALE

SCAFELL

6 – 1926   5 – 1914

8 – 1938

LANGDALE

CHAPEL STILE

WASTWATER

EAST BUTTRESS

To AMBLESIDE

Lakeland's Great Routes

No.	Year	Route Name	Grade	Location	Pioneer's Name	Climbers' Comment
10)	1940	Eagle Front	VS	Eagle Crag, Buttermere	W. Peascod	A great route.
	1941	Suaviter	MS	Grey Crag, Buttermere	W. Peascod	Very pleasing.
		Resurrection Route	VS	High Crag, Buttermere	W. Peascod	Climbed in nails in the rain.
	1945	Great Central Climb	VS	Esk Buttress	R. J. Birkett	Attempts the centre of this buttress.
	1946	White Ghyll Wall	MVS	White Ghyll	R. J. Birkett	Fine exposure.
	1946	Honister Wall	HS	Buckstone Howe	W. Peascod	Steep on good hoods.
	1946	Falconer's Crack	VS	Eagle Crag, Borrowdale	W. Peascod	Superb route—first on the crag.
	1947	Slip Knot	MVS	White Ghyll	R. J. Birkett	A remarkable solution.
		Leopard's Crawl	HVS	Dow Crag	R. J. Birkett	First graded severe.
	1948	Haste Not	VS	White Ghyll	R. J. Birkett	Great exposure, great climbing.
11)	1948	Slab & Groove	HVS	Scafell	R. J. Birkett	Remarkable contrast.
		Kipling Groove	HVS	Gimmer Crag	A. R. Dolphin	A new generation.
	1948	Dale Head Pillar	MVS	Dale Head, Newlands	W. Peascod	Again a new crag opened up.
	1949	Perhaps Not	HVS	White Ghyll	R. J. Birkett	Very serious and hard.
		Do Not	HVS	White Ghyll	R. J. Birkett	Very serious and hard.
12)	1949	Harlot Face	E1	Castle Rock	R. J. Birkett	The first Extreme.
13)	1951	Deer Bield Buttress	E1	Deer Bield, Easedale	A. R. Dolphin	Good, long and hard.
		Ferrous Buttress	HVS	Iron Crag, Thirlmere	A. R. Dolphin	Thankfully unique!
	1952	Hell's Groove	E1	East Buttress, Scafell	A. R. Dolphin, P. Greenwood led first pitch	Ferocious.
	1952	Cleopatra	HVS	Buckstone Howe	W. Peascod	Technical, bold, superb.

	Year	Route	Grade	Crag	First ascent	Description
	1953	Communist Convert	VS	Raven Crag, Thirlmere	A. R. Dolphin	A quality route on a new crag.
14)	1958	Golden Slipper	HVS	Gimmer Crag	A. Austin	Very pleasant.
	1960	Astra	E2	Pavey Ark	A. Austin	A brilliant solution.
	1962	Arcturus	HVS	Pavey Ark	A. Austin	Very popular.
	1963	Gimmer String	E1	Gimmer Crag	A. Austin	Enjoyable climbing up steep rock.
	1964	Man of Straw	E1	White Ghyll	A. Austin	Very delicate.
		Gandalf's Groove	E1	Neckband Crag, Langdale	A. Austin	Nice climbing.
	1965	Carnival	E1	Eagle Crag, Buttermere	A. Austin with Roper Soper	Thoroughly good.
	1966	Chimney Variant	E2	White Ghyll	A. Austin	Exposed and technical.
		Razor Crack	E1	Neckband Crag	A. Austin	Strenuous jamming—a feast.
	1970	Brackenclock	E2	Pavey Ark	A. Austin	Steep but pleasant.
	1971	Haste Not Direct	E2	White Ghyll	A. Austin	One of the finest.
15)	1974	Footless Crow	E5(6b)	Goat Crag, Borrowdale	P. Livesey	A new dimension.
		Bitter Oasis	E3(6a, 6a)	Goat Crag, Borrowdale	P. Livesey	Sustained and very popular.
		Dry Gasp	E4(6a)	Upper Falcon Crag, Borrowdale	P. Livesey	Sustained with little protection.
	1976	Lost Colonies	E3(6a)	High Crag, Buttermere	P. Livesey	Highly technical.
	1977	Lost Horizons	E4(6a,5c)	East Buttress, Scafell	P. Livesey	The Great overhanging corner/groove.
	1978	Das Kapital	E4(6b,6b)	Raven Crag, Thirlmere	P. Livesey shared with P. Gomersal	Constantly overhanging.

2

Walter Parry Haskett-Smith
(1859–1946)

It was no accident that a very young classics scholar and Oxford graduate, along with a party of friends and students, took rooms at Dan Tyson's of Wasdale Head. Carefully studying maps of England and finally the ordnance survey map of Cumberland, Walter Parry Haskett-Smith selected Wasdale with the intention of reading hard and walking hard.

From 18th July to 10th August 1881, the party did just that. But then, over the last three days of their holiday, the remarkable happened. They found a new way up the Pillar Rock, accompanied by F. H. Bowring, an enthusiastic fell walker, the team being W.P.H.S., F. H. Bowring, J. A. Hamilton and W. Bartlett.

H.S. went on to solo a way up Scafell by a gully on the Eskdale side. Finally he climbed the face of Lingmell Crags to the cairn from Piers Ghyll, accompanied by J. A. Hamilton. These were hard scrambles, involving a great deal of danger and considerable exposure and requiring athletic ability to pull and jump up grass ledges and steep, broken rocks. They had departed from fell walking and undertaken something quite different. It was not yet, however, true rock climbing. Haskett-Smith had been the instigator and the leader. Indeed, he achieved one of the ascents unaccompanied. It was already apparent that this man was somebody out of the ordinary.

He had first visited the British hills the year before, in 1880, when, along with another university reading party, he had spent a month in Snowdonia. This had a profound effect upon him and when, the following year, a similar party was conceived, his friends requested him to select the location. His choice of Wasdale could not have been more suitable. His companions were I. G. Hamilton of Balliol College, Oxford, afterwards Lord Sumnar Bartlett of Corpus; H. B. Simpson of Magdalen, Oxford, and (a son of Lord Bowen the judge) W. E. Bowen of Balliol College. The latter, Mrs Thomas Tyson, proprietress of the Wasdale establishment at which they were staying, referred to as "lahl chop" ("little chap"), much to his great disgust. He was smaller than the rest of his companions and was consequently given a greater share of Mrs Tyson's famous Cumbrian hospitality.

Born in 1859, W. P. Haskett-Smith was educated at Eton and from there went to Trinity College, Oxford. In 1880 he obtained a degree in classic moderations. The following year, when at Wasdale, he was reading for a degree in Literae Humaniores, which two years later he passed with honours. In later life he became a barrister and philologist. He was called to the Bar at Lincoln's Inn, though strangely he never practised, and he once had a fierce row with a friend and solicitor who, in good faith, sent him a brief.

It was not for these achievements, however, that he became famous. At school and later at university he was noted more for his amazing athletic prowess than for his academic success. When a schoolboy at Eton he climbed a high wall on one side of the playing fields—it was a 'first ascent'. He broke the Oxford long-jump record with a distance of 25½ feet. Unfortunately this was in practice only, and he was never accredited the record.

Fortunately, when at Wasdale, at the age of twenty-two he met Frederick H. Bowring, who was fifty-eight and a keen and experienced fell walker. It was just the fuel that Haskett-Smith required. Bowring introduced him to the fells around Wasdale, showing him the established tracks and paths, the ways to the summit and to the crags, and told him what was done and what was not. By the end of the month Haskett-Smith knew his vocation, and those three scrambles marked the beginning of an era and the birth of a new sport—the sport of rock climbing.

At this time, 1881, there was a growing and flourishing tourist industry. The Lakes became very popular and relatively accessible due to the advent of the railway. A number of 'Alpinists' also visited Wasdale merely to obtain out-of-season practice for the larger mountains. Walking and traversing the hills and summits was a frequent activity. Even so, rock climbing as a sport in its own right was unknown; up to this time the 'easy way' had always been sought.

Samuel Coleridge had descended Broad Stand in the previous century because it was the shortest link from Scafell to Mickledore and hence to Scafell Pike (the highest mountain in England). Having got down the initial easy section, he had become 'trapped' and, unable to ascend, was forced to continue his descent. He finally reached Mickledore (the narrow ridge between the two Scafells) by making some frightening jumps down rock walls and ledges. (Today, as then, Broadstand is a very serious place for the ordinary walker and should be tackled only by very competent parties. A slip usually results in a long fall down the Eskdale side of the Mickledore gap. There are incidents, often serious, on this piece of rock every year.) This event, it is said, so influenced Wordsworth that he wrote 'The Brothers' about the Pillar Rock above Ennerdale:

> You see precipice;—it wears the shape
> Of a vast building made of many crags;
> And in the midst is one particular rock
> That rises like a column from the vale,
> Whence by our shepherds it is called, The Pillar.

This immediately drew attention to and advertised the Pillar Rock. Pillar is unique in Lakeland summits in that it is a mountain that cannot be reached by ordinary fell walking. Like an alpine peak, it can be gained only by climbing, albeit of an easy standard. Nevertheless it was a sought-after prize, and much has been written of its early ascents and ascensionists. These early adventurers, based in Wasdale Head, formed a group of people intent on gaining Pillar's summit. They came to be known as 'the Pillarites'.

The Pillar Rock then was first climbed in 1826 by J. Atkinson, who was a local shepherd. His route is known as the 'Old West'. It was a bold scramble, and it was not until 1863 that another route was discovered to gain the summit. This was known as the 'Slab and Notch' climb.

By 1872 there were four different ways up, the latter two being the 'Old Wall Route' and 'Pendlebury Traverse'. These were rock climbs, but they were done purely to gain the summit and not for their own merits.

In the summer of 1892, and a year after his first visit, Haskett-Smith returned to Wasdale Head, this time accompanied by his brother. He produced seven new rock climbs. These climbs were done for their own sake with no pretence of merely being ways to the summit. They lay on Scafell Crag above Wasdale, Great End above Borrowdale, Pillar Rock in Ennerdale, Pavey Ark and Gimmer Crag in Langdale. It was a most impressive start to the new sport. He had discovered the joy and fascination that come with new adventure. Today the climbs are graded Moderate and Difficult. They are undoubtedly easy by present-day standards but are real rock climbs. Indeed, West Jordan climbs on Pillar Rock still taxes the inexperienced climber.

Haskett-Smith did not revisit the Lakes for two years, for in 1883 he climbed in the Pyrenees, but on his return to the Lake District he produced another five new routes. Steep Ghyll on Scafell was undoubtedly the hardest; it was graded Severe and has an evil reputation for being loose and wet. However, the most significant was the Needle Ridge on the Napes rocks, Great Gable, for it was from this climb that he reconnoitred the Napes Needle, the most famous rock climb of all!

On Steep Ghyll he had been accompanied by John W. Robinson of Lorton, Cockermouth. This partnership formed a very strong climbing team. Robinson had been introduced to Haskett-Smith by Bowring, and he was a formidable mountain man. He frequently rose at 4 a.m. and from his home at Lorton walked to Wasdale Head. There he would meet with a party of climbers, have a full day of hard climbing and then tramp home apparently as "fresh and vigorous" as when he had started.

Later Robinson became a very popular figure at Wasdale.

Indeed, he accompanied J. Norman Collie on the first ascent of Moss Ghyll on Scafell when the infamous 'Collies Step' was cut. Moss Ghyll had been attempted by a number of parties, all of whom had failed at a point two-thirds of the way up the gully. They were stopped by a gigantic chockstone (a large stone 'choking' the gully) which overhung the gully floor. The only way past this obstacle lay up the sides of the gully. Unfortunately the right gully wall was overhanging and the left-hand wall just less than vertical. Tackling the left-hand wall, Collie brought science in to aid his progress and chipped a foothold in the rock with an ice-axe. This enabled the party to bypass the obstacle and so climb the gully for the first time. This is recognized as the first use of an 'artificial' aid in climbing, and it created much controversy. As is the way with these things, people criticized Collie's action but still ascended the gully, making full use of this 'illegal' hold. It was a logical deed for a man of his background.

Professor Collie was an important and distinguished scientist. He was the first man to discover neon and the first to take X-ray photographs.

Robinson was most certainly a vital and colourful character. Apparently he always wore a yellow tweed suit, was well built and bald and had sandy whiskers and merry blue eyes. He accompanied Collie in the Himalayas, but it was for his local knowledge of the Lake District that he was most revered. Haskett-Smith said of him: "What number of climbers there must be to whom the essence of Lake Country climbing was John Robinson."

When Robinson died in 1907, Haskett-Smith directed a number of his friends to build a cairn at the end of the high-level route to Pillar, for it was Robinson who first trod that famous track. Near the cairn on a rock face there is a plaque whose inscription reads, "For the Remembrance of J.W.R. by W.H. in Lorton."

It was Robinson's local knowledge that led Haskett-Smith to his first sight of that splendid thumb of rock the Napes Needle. His father had discovered and sketched it as far back as 1828 in one of his outings across the Wasdale face of Great Gable. One day, after a storm, Robinson took Haskett-Smith to the Needle. A lucky combination of bright sunshine and great cloud mass showed the profile of the Needle to its best effect. It inspired him to go back and attempt to climb it at the earliest opportunity.

Robinson was equally impressed and said in a hushed voice, "Would a Swiss guide attempt a thing like that?"

It was from the Needle Ridge then that Haskett-Smith inspected the Needle and assessed the possibilities of climbing it. It was two years later, however, in 1886, that the opportunity arose. He was somewhat hampered by lack of companions—of course there were no clubs or organized groups, and he often had to climb solo or with his contemporaries at university. Understandably they were often less keen than he to risk life and limb rock climbing. This led to the complaint that he often had to "waste on a mere walk a day of glorious climbing weather". The result was that many of his climbs and new routes were done solo, without companions or rope, and this made them even more remarkable.

One such day was 27th June 1885. He walked down Wasdale with some friends who were ending their holiday and returning home. Suffering from an acute headache he returned to the hotel at Wasdale Head with an afternoon still to spare. Deciding to walk it off, he made his way from the hotel towards the Napes. He found himself approaching the Needle.

By this time my headache had gone and the Needle itself had a more attractive look about it. The main trouble lay in the cracks and crevices which were tightly packed with small stones flush with the surface of the slabs and thatched with slippery grass. The prospect from the shoulder was not encouraging. The Lingmell face of the top block was covered with a brown brittle lichen which concealed whatever holds there might be and if the top of the block were rounded things looked hopeless. The only test of this was to throw up a stone and, if it stayed there, it would be proof that the roof was fairly flat. Diligent search revealed only two stones on the shoulder, one the size of a snuffbox, the other nearly as big as a brick. The little one bounded off and was lost; but the other big one behaved better and encouraged me to follow it. There was no means of recording my visit except a small boss near to the North edge of the stone round which my handkerchief was tied with my brick on the top of it to keep it from being blown away. The descent was somewhat unnerving, as the lichen dust concealed all the little footholds, but all went well. Below the shoulder I had half a mind to try the opposite side to that of my ascent.

This was a most remarkable achievement, a feat of tremendous courage and daring. It was a fitting prize for the self-confident, strongly individualistic man who from his first visit to Wasdale had wished to rock climb pure and simple, to climb for its thrill and adventure and for the physical and nervous satisfaction in mastering it.

Today the Napes Needle is graded Very Difficult, and it is with some interest that the climber mantelshelfs onto a notch in the top block, precariously stands up, makes a delicate traverse left and finally moves up to the very top, all the time conscious of the fact that every move has to be reversed and that the ground lies eighty feet below with nothing but space between him and it. (The mantelshelf is a type of move in rock climbing where the hands are placed on a narrow ledge and where the feet or knees must be moved up and placed beside your hands. It requires good technique and a sound sense of balance.)

Rock climbing could now truly be described as a sport in its own right. It owed nothing to Alpinism or walking the fells. It stood on its own merits. For many a whole new way of life had been born.

Haskett-Smith did many more new ascents in the Lake District. He also climbed and travelled extensively abroad, in the Alps, Norway, Spain and the Pyrenees, North Africa, Greece, the Balkans, the Rockies and the Andes.

Probably the most notable of his Lakeland ascents came in 1891, when he finally managed to complete the north climb (Difficult) on Pillar Rock. He had tried this climb repeatedly over a ten-year period and up till then had always been defeated by the steepening of the cliff which extends from the north-west corner of Low Man eastward to the nose overhanging Savage Gully. It must have been a psychological barrier, because the climb is somewhat easier than the Napes Needle, although it may have had more vegetation and loose rock than is evident today. In fact, Haskett-Smith was almost killed on one of the attempts, when a large block, which he was climbing around, parted company with the cliff and crashed to the screes below. Fortunately he was able to secure a hold and stop himself from falling. It had, however, been a very close shave. Another factor which may have had a bearing on the matter was the length of the route: the north climb is 320 feet long, while the Needle is a mere 80 feet.

Very widely read and highly educated, Haskett-Smith was known as a great conversationalist and raconteur. He had a fine sense of humour and appreciated the local Cumberland characters and dialect. One such character, Will Ritson, was the landlord of the Huntsman's Inn at Wasdale (now known as the 'Wasdale Head') during these early pioneering days. He described Wasdale as having "the highest mountain, the deepest lake, the smallest church and the biggest liar in England". He was absolutely correct on all counts: Scafell Pike is the highest mountain in England, Wastwater the deepest lake, and he himself was undoubtedly the biggest liar.

The following extract written by Haskett-Smith shows all the above qualities admirably:

Auld Will was a tall, gaunt, long man with unusually long arms, which, like those of Rob Roy, were a source of great pride to their owner. They figured largely in a comical scene which left an indelible impression on my mind. A wagonette from one of the coast towns had brought up a party of six or seven people, who were wandering about the valley, leaving one of their number behind who was so much over awed by the unwanted sternness of the surrounding hills that he never ventured to quit the Inn yard till his friends returned. This was a timid little man, thin and narrow chested, wearing a threadbare frock coat and a rusty top hat. He was the very picture drawn by Calverley:

> He stood, a worn out city clerk,
> Who'd toiled and seen no holiday,
> For forty years from dawn to dark,
> Alone beside Carmarthen Bay.

Meanwhile Ritson had been drinking in the bar-room, and with startling suddenness came reeling forth in the direction of the "Worn out city clerk". He was in the best of good humours, but no stranger would have guessed it. He had forgotten his hat and coat, and looked half cannibal and half Beserker. Ever vain of his long arms, he was wont in moments of exhilaration to display them by executing a horrifying war dance. The main feature of this performance was to shoot out both arms horizontally, then suddenly bending the body sideways from the hips, to bring the finger tips of one hand nearly to the ground, then, with an equally rapid reverse whirl, to bend over the other way and bring the other hand down on the other side. This manoeuvre repeated half a dozen times with lightning speed, made him look like an inebriated windmill, and in this guise he bore down upon the inoffensive visitor, roaring out, "Art a wrostler?" It was a sight to daunt the stoutest heart. The little man was well-nigh paralysed, but luckily misunderstanding the question as an enquiry for the ostler, stammered, "N-n-no Sir, I think I saw him over there", and pointing towards the stables, he made a slight quick movement in the same direction. This was lucky for him. At that moment Ritson made a wild clutch at him, missed his mark and, finding himself several yards down the lane, before he could recover his balance, wisely made no effort to turn back. The little man was saved and sank down gasping on to the nearest seat.

A further illustration of Haskett-Smith's wit and calibre was evident on Easter Sunday 1936, for on that day he again climbed Napes Needle, fifty years after he had made the first ascent. He was seventy-six years old, and the previous day he had also spent climbing, on Pillar Rock. Hundreds of people had gathered round the Needle, and when he reached the top, there was a burst of spontaneous applause. Someone yelled from the crowd, "Tell us a story," and he shouted back, "There is no other story. This is the top storey."

He frequently wrote articles for journals and magazines and in 1894 his *Climbing in the British Isles, Volume I, England* was published. It was intended that there should be three volumes, England, Wales and Scotland. A second volume was published, but this was about Ireland. The books were not a commercial success, and the others were never published. Volume I is a delightful little book, available until quite recently, very informative and charmingly produced. It was of course the very first rock-climbing guide to England.

Kent, the garden of England, meant a lot to Haskett-Smith; it was there where he was born in 1859 on the family estate of Trowswell near Goudhurst. He often referred to it as "our part of the country". Forced out of his house there due to bomb damage, he moved to Parkstone in Dorset. On 11th March 1946, aged eighty-six years, preceded two months earlier by his brother and also considerably upset at having to leave his native Kent, he died.

Although President of the Fell & Rock Climbers Club from 1901 to 1903 and also a member of the Alpine Club, he never really associated with any particular mountain group. He climbed for the best reason of all—the fun of it. He loved its individual adventure and the qualities of judgement and iron nerve it requires.

Haskett-Smith said of F. H. Bowring, the man who purely by

chance he met that first summer at Wasdale, "Climbing owes more to him than any other man." This was true insofar as he was introduced to the Fells by Bowring, but it is Haskett-Smith who can, without challenge, be called 'the Father of Rock Climbing'.

	Route name	*Grade*	*Location*	*Comments*
1882	Deep Ghyll	M	Scafell	
	Central Gully	M	Great End	
	South East Gully	M		
	Central Jordan Climb	D	Pillar Rock	
	West Jordan Climb	D	Pillar Rock	
	Great Gully	D	Pavey Ark	
	North West Gully		Gimmer Crag	
1884	East Jordan Climb		Pillar Rock	
	High Man from Jordan Gap	M	Scafell Pinnacle	
	Steep Ghyll	S	Scafell	
	Low Man, High Man		Scafell	
	Needle Ridge	D	The Napes	solo
1886	The Needle	D	The Napes	solo
	Little Gully	M	Pavey Ark	
	E Buttress—Left Hand Route	M	Dow	
1887	The Great Chimney	D	Pillar Rock	
	The Arete	M		
	The Curtain	D		
1888	High Man via Steep & Slingsby Chimney	S	Scafell Pinnacle	W. Cecil Slingsby led
	Great Gully	HD	Dow	G. Hastings led
1889	Sphinx Rock	D	The Napes	
1891	North Climb	D	Pillar Rock	At last!
1893	Petty's Rift		Scafell	
1908	Haskett Gully	S	Pillar Rock	

3
Owen Glynne Jones
(2nd November 1867–28th August 1899)

Regarded as an enigma, this man has engendered more contradictory stories than any other Lakeland pioneer. He always asserted that his initials, O.G.J., stood for the "Only Genuine Jones". This is typical Jones, poignant yet apt, for there most certainly could be no man quite like him.

Jones really shocked the upper-middle-class Victorian climbing scene. He awoke them to completely new ideas and concepts of difficulty. Forceful and brilliant, he saw absolutely no reason to hide these qualities. He talked often of his virtues and featured in newspapers, magazines etc, giving frequent interviews. In fact, his whole dynamic career can be closely paralleled by those of some modern-day pioneers.

Ascents of Kern Knotts Crack (MVS) and Jones's Route Direct (S) up the Pinnacle Face of Scafell were tremendous steps forward in commitment and difficulty. His route direct up the Pinnacle Face was not repeated for fourteen years and was the scene of a most horrific accident in 1903. At the time both routes were graded Exceptionally Severe by Jones. This grade, and the present-day system of grading the difficulty of British climbs, was invented by him.

A Welshman by blood, Jones was a Londoner by birth, born on 2nd November 1867 in Clarendon Street, Paddington. His father was a carpenter and builder. At school he distinguished himself in science and won several prizes. Awarded a scholarship, he passed to the technical college at Finsbury, where he obtained a Cloth-works Scholarship to the Central Institution. His teacher spoke highly of him: "He is imbued with modern methods . . . and is possessed of a healthy enthusiasm for his work that is infectious." Three years were spent in the engineering department, and at the end he obtained the highest position in the class list of any student of his year. He went on the following year to a first-class honours BSc in experimental physics at London University (1890) and later accepted the post of physics master at the City of London School.

He was first inspired to visit Lakeland and the Cumbrian Fells when he sighted a photograph of the Napes Needle in London.

> I have a vivid recollection of walking down the Strand one wet Spring afternoon in 1891, oppressed with the commonplace London streets and the flatness of people and things in general, and crossing over by sheer force of habit to Spooners Photograph shop. In the centre of the window, and eclipsing to my perverted vision every other object around it, was a striking enlargement from the original half-plate of Dixon's Needle. I heard a by-stander at my elbow draw his friends attention to the figures in the picture with the remark "Scott! what fools". But that evening a copy of the Needle hung in my room; in a fortnight Easter had come round and I found myself on top of the Pinnacle.

On the ascent Jones and his companion, Dr W. E. Sumpner, had to be assisted initially to get up and then to get down by Professor Collie, who had himself just climbed the Needle. It was typical of Jones that, with no experience, no nails in his boots and basically no idea, he had been inspired by that photograph. His raw enthusiasm and ambition had carried him up, and if Collie had not been available, then I am sure something else would have prevailed!

It was in 1892 that Jones pioneered his first new route, but East Pisgah Chimney on Pillar Rock was a mere scramble, and it gave no indication of what was to follow. He was, however, rapidly ticking off existing routes and the previous summer had had a useful and energetic season in the Alps. All the time learning the craft, he steadily gained technique to match his boundless enthusiasm and ambition.

The first breakthrough came in November 1893, when he ascended Sergeant Crag Chimney (HS) with that local expert John Robinson. This had a pitch of considerable difficulty, and it was the first of Jones's Exceptionally Severe courses. The climb lies high up the Langstrath Valley and is reached from the village of Stonethwaite in Borrowdale. Sergeant Crag is large, high and very infrequently visited; the valley has an atmosphere that is rarely found in the more popular areas. Below lies the Gash Rock, an interesting boulder of sizeable proportions, and the superb swimming-pools of the Langstrath Beck.

Sergeant Crag Gully was one of my very first rock climbs. My father took me to the crag, and we ascended the climb with water streaming down the rocks and oozing out of the considerable vegetation. It was real adventure, and we both found the crux fourth pitch difficult under the prevailing conditions. It is one of the very few rock climbs that I have done twice, and I remember that sometime later I had a craze for climbing the 'classic gullies' in pouring rain. One such day saw me at the foot of Sergeant Crag Gully, where a wet-suit and flippers would have been more appropriate than anorak and climbing boots. Anyhow, my companion, Cliff Brown, and I managed the climb and emerged at the top absolutely saturated. Down in the valley bottom the beck was in considerable spate. We flung off our sodden clothes and jumped in. Washed down waterfalls and through pools at considerable speed, we passed a party of ramblers walking up the bank. Clad in bright orange cagoules and with every conceivable survival aid strapped to their backs, they obviously thought we were lunatics. It was a fitting end to a great day out, and we thought that O. G. Jones would have been proud of us!

The same year that he climbed Sergeant's Crag Gully, Jones put up Kern Knotts Chimney (D). It was from there that he longingly looked down the formidable Kern Knotts Crack. Robinson thought it impossible, and told him so, but Jones thought differently and was not to be intimidated. It was some two years before he was to return to Wasdale.

Summer 1894 saw Jones in the Alps, the Engadine and the Dolomites. The following year he was to climb with Haskett-Smith in Wales. In the Cader Idris they did first ascents of East and Great Gully on Craig Cau. Later he again visited the Alps and climbed extensively.

At Christmas 1895 he was back at the beloved Wasdale Head Hotel, and it was there that he met Ashley Abraham. It was a most significant meeting, for the Abraham brothers were to shape Jones's rock-climbing career for the rest of his life.

Their father was a professional photographer with a shop in Keswick. George and Ashley were their names, and they became the first professional rock-climbing photographers. With an unbelievably heavy and bulky wooden-plate camera, they recorded for posterity the most wonderful action shots and mountain scenes. Fine climbers, they loved the mountains and photographed all over Britain and the Alps. By the time Jones met them, they had pioneered a number of routes, including Walla Crag Gully, the first climb done in Borrowdale.

These two Keswick brothers had experience and enthusiasm, but more significantly they knew the importance of rope technique. It is said that they developed the science of rope management and invented the fundamental safety factor in climbing—that of belaying. (Belaying is the act of tying oneself to the rock using the rope, e.g. looping the rope around a flake and securing with an appropriate knot.) It hardly seems credible now but many climbers of their day would simply tie themselves together and all climb at once or, if one remained stationary, merely stand on an appropriate ledge with the rope completely unattached to the rock! This was very primitive and potentially lethal, as will be seen later.

The Abrahams' company was a giant inspiration to Jones; it also consolidated his technique and acted as a stabilizing influence. George went on to write a number of fine books on mountaineering, and Ashley, the younger brother, wrote guides to Wales and Skye.

It was the following Easter, 1896, that Jones called at the Abrahams' shop in Keswick. George Abrahams wrote in *Mountain Adventures at Home and Abroad*: "Without any forward he called on us in the early hours of a beautiful April morning, after a long night journey from town. In two hours' time mutual keenness had promoted friendship, parental misgiving had been overcome, and we were off to Wasdale."

They met John Robinson at Sty Head and proceeded to the Napes Area of Great Gable. In 1¾ hours the party of four ascended Eagle's Nest Ridge, the Needle, the Needle Ridge and the Arrowhead Ridge and descended the Needle Gully twice. "Yet the first day with Owen Glynne Jones meant much more than wrestling with those glorious crags, every muscle and sense alive to instant action as to method of rope and rock work, our real selves stood revealed and a friendship was formed which proved in after years to be the most valuable possession of life," wrote George. Ashley and George were twenty and twenty-four years old respectively, Jones twenty-eight.

On their way to the Napes they passed under that clean and compact little crag known as Kern Knotts. They stopped and looked awfully at the vertical rift of the Kern Knotts Crack. Robinson said: "Well, Jones, if you climb that crack, I'll never speak to you again!"

The team of Jones and the Abrahams soon made their mark, for on 20th April 1886 they pioneered their first new route together. The line was appealing, a curving crack from the depths of a great gully to the summit ridge of the mighty Scafell. The route was, of course, 'Scafell Pinnacle by Jones Route from Deep Ghyll' (Mild Severe). It was also the Abrahams' first attempt at action photography. They had mounted their colossal camera on the traverse the other side of Deep Ghyll, and much toing and froing was necessary to get a satisfactory exposure. Jones wrote: "Our time up from Lord's Rake had been slow—something like four hours—but much had been spent with photography and in reconnoitring. Another day, two years later, I managed it in less than half the time."

Two days later they tackled Collier's Climb (D) again on Scafell. This climb had built up a formidable reputation and lay unrepeated for three years. Here Jones, prompted by George and Ashley, had them untie his rope. He took in the loose end and then lowered it behind some small chockstones jammed in a crack in front of him. They caught the lowered end and again secured him. Jones had now effected a running belay using only the rope and natural chockstones. Modern-day climbers secure themselves by running belays using just this principle. The difference is that nowadays the chockstones are artificially made of aluminium and inserted into cracks, and the rope is clipped into them, using karabiners—the leading man does not have to untie.

Jones wrote of this incident and also of how he used combined tactics to overcome the climb:

> However steady a young man may be, there are times when his friends think him weak in the head, such a time was this, and I anxiously asked him if he could hold it perfectly still while I used it. 'You may do anything except waltz on it,' was the encouraging rejoinder, and I promptly placed my left foot on his parietal. 'That's all right' the tough young head called out, 'You may stay there all day if you like.' This was reassuring, but I had come out to climb and meant to move on. . . . Casting around for some means of anchoring on my own rope, I saw that in a crack to my right a bunch of small stones were firmly jammed, and that day light could be seen behind them down a hole that pointed through to the Progress fifteen feet below. . . . Calling them to let go the rope, I drew up the free end by my teeth and my 'unemployed' hand, and let it fall straight down the hole to them. If a fall occurred now in trying the next few feet I could only tumble three or four yards, and should not pass over my friends' heads and the Rake's Progress. . . . Now was the time to appreciate the joy of climbing, in perfect health, with perfect weather, and in a difficult place without danger, and I secretly laughed as I called to the others that the outlook was terribly bad and that our enterprise must be given up. But they also laughed and told me to go higher and change my mind, for they knew by the time that my temper was unruffled.

What would Jones not have done given modern equipment and knowledge!

Christmas arrived along with a biting wind, iced-up rocks and Jones. They tackled the Shamrock Gully on Pillar Rocks (S). George Abraham relates the incident:

> About 25 feet above us no progress was made for some time, and after considerable delay we called up to him inquiringly. No answer came; but at last the oppressive silence was broken by the words; 'I cannot get up or down safely!' The position was alarming for the jaws of the gully dipped deeply below, and, though the rope was secured to us and the great boulders, a fall would have been serious. A few moments later Jones, with remarkable foresight and judgement, espied a small piece of jutting rock no bigger than the top of an egg-cup. This was just above him on the right, but it was possible to

swing the rope up to and over it; and he began the ascent thus secured. We paid the rope out from the cave and all went well for a time. Then suddenly there was a cry of warning, and something of a more solid nature appeared. 'Hold tight!' was the startled shout, and Jones came swinging in pendulum fashion across the wall with startling impetus. The rope held over the belay, and he crashed pell-mell amongst us in the bed of the cave. We collapsed like nine-pins, sprawling in all directions. In the mêlée the rope flew out of my hand, and I well remember how Jones sat up presently on the snow, rubbing his bruises and accusing me of losing my head and the rope simultaneously.

They eventually climbed the pitch and the route by combined tactics, the Abrahams forming a human pyramid. Their 'indomitable leader' carried on despite driving sleet and oncoming darkness. Finally they abseiled down to the Shamrock traverse in total darkness. The high-level route was iced up, and they roped together for safety. Typically Jones lost his way, and they did not reach the Wasdale Head until midnight.

The year 1897 was one of Jones's most notable. He pioneered C Gully on the Screes (MVS), Central Chimney (S) on Dow Crag, Kern Knotts West Chimney (D) and the incredible Kern Knotts Crack (MVS), both on Great Gable.

The C Gully on the Screes and the Central Chimney on Dow Crag were formidable gully and chimney climbs, certainly the hardest of their day. Central Chimney developed a frightening reputation as the most dangerous climb in the area. Although 'C' Gully is harder, Central Chimney looks formidable even by modern standards! A steep, curving crack with an overhanging wall on the left and a steep, horribly smooth and frictionless wall on the right, it is steep and insecure. When Jones climbed it, there was no adequate protection from the rope, and it would be full of loose rock. It has to be climbed by jamming the hands in the crack while bridging with the feet up the wall on the right. More than one climber today finds himself slipping unstoppably to the ground after gaining thirty feet or so.

Kern Knotts Crack was a breakthrough in concept. Thought impossible by many until Jones climbed it, it remains a precarious piece of climbing. Not really a chimney, definitely not a gully, it is more of a steep crack splitting a plumb vertical wall. As such it was a breakthrough in climbing history. Until its ascent, with of course a few exceptions, climbs were made in gullies or chimneys. A climber could feel much more secure, with rope technique as it was then, inside the confining walls of a chimney. Jones altered that and started a new climbing era.

The following year produced the magnificent 'Jones's Route Direct from Lord's Rake' (S), climbed during his Easter holiday. Truly a wall climb, it wandered up the main face of the Scafell Pinnacle. It was a 'thin' piece of climbing. With G. T. Walker he accomplished the climb in stockinged feet, as he considered nailed boots (of that period) inadequate for use on the steep, holdless slabs. It required fine balance and a great concentration of mind to force himself up the ever-steepening and overlapping slabs for two hundred feet. The party had already been climbing for most of the day. Jones wrote:

In spite of the late hour I could not refrain from a trial trip on the edge of the great Low Man Buttress. At the point where the earlier party found the direct ascent barred by smooth ice on the wall, [a reference to an attempt by C. Hopkinson and party in 1887] and decided to traverse off to the gully on the left, we had a council of war. It resulted in my throwing down my boots to Walker, and then crawling up fifty feet of, perhaps, the steepest and smoothest slabs to which I have ever trusted myself. This brought me to a tiny corner where I essayed to haul in the rope attached to my companion. But he also had to remove his boots and traverse to a point vertically below me before he could follow up in safety. We were now some distance to the left of the edge of Deep Ghyll, and straight up above us we could distinguish the crack where our new route was to terminate. Getting Walker to lodge firmly in a notch somewhat larger than mine, six foot away on the steep Ghyll side, I went off again up another forty foot of smooth rock, aided by a zigzagging crack an inch or so in width, that supplied lodgement for the toes, and a moderate grip for the finger-tips. After both had arrived thus far, we were able, with extreme care, to reach the side wall of the nose itself, and at a point perhaps fifty feet from its crest we turned round its main outside buttress and found ourselves in a spacious chamber with a flat floor and a considerable roof, the first and only genuine resting place worthy of the name, that we found along our route. We could look straight down Hopkinson's Gully, and would gladly have descended into it and passed the time of day with a little speculative scrambling thereabouts. But darkness was coming on apace, and we had yet a most awkward corner to negotiate before finishing our appointed business.

Standing on Walker's shoulders I screwed myself out at the right-hand top corner of our waiting-room, and started along a traverse across the right face of the nose. The toes of the feet were in a horizontal crack, the heels had no support, and the hands no grip. It was only by pressing the body close to the wall, which was fortunately a few degrees from the perpendicular, and by sliding the feet along almost inch by inch, that the operation could be effected. It was with no small sense of relief that the end was reached in a few yards, and a narrow vertical fissure entered that gave easy access to the top of the nose. Then we put our boots on again and hurried. . . .

It is thus possible to reach the summit of the Scafell Pinnacle by a route up the buttress quite independent of either of the great walls that flank it.

His supremacy as the finest rock climber of his day now remained unchallenged. The route was not tried again until 21st September 1903. A party of four, men consisting of R. W. Broadrick, Henry Jupp, Stanley Ridsdale and A. E. W. Garrett, was stretched out across the face when Garrett fell. Each one in turn was plucked off as they were all connected by a rope. Three were killed instantly, and Ridsdale died a few hours later. A most tragic accident, it had a devastating effect upon the climbing fraternity. The route waited a further nine years before it was attempted again.

Jones's summer holiday was spent in the Alps. Here he was beginning to excel. He frequently climbed two peaks a day and once did three. When Christmas 1888 arrived, a superbly fit Jones was back at Wasdale Head, his prime objective the awesome Walker's Gully on Pillar Rock. This gully splits the Shamrock from Pillar Rock itself. It is a very steep, black and rather impressive rip in otherwise unbroken cliff.

The weather was appalling, and George Abraham wrote:

The Christmas of 1898 was marked by heavy rain and unreasonable conditions. Several large parties of climbers had come to the hotel and, after a day or two of smoking and grumbling, had departed; until, at the New Year, Mr. Jones and myself were the only climbers left there. To keep ourselves in training we struggled up through the powdery snow of the Central Gully on Gable Crag, performed many rash feats at the end of the barn and the billiard table, besides leaving a considerable quantity of our clothing on the 'Mosedale Boulder'.

Abraham and Jones walked up and inspected the top of the

gully. They found that the top scree funnel was firmly bound with snow and ice. This was a fillip despite the previously poor weather because in summer this easy-angled top section is piled with loose scree and there are frequent stone falls into the gully with potentially murderous capability. Jones, lowered to the edge by George Abraham, reported on seeing "icy, overhanging rock and the mist filled abyss far below", but he thought there was a chance.

By 7th January 1899 the weather had not improved. A. E. Field, a friend and respected third man, had arrived at the hotel, and they decided it had to be done despite the weather. It was raining and sleeting when they set off, but by the time they reached the snow-line and the foot of the gully, it had eased off.

The ascent was a major feat of determination, skill and resilience against pain and fear. Jones finished climbing the most difficult section up wet ice in stockinged feet, after many hours in freezing, wet conditions. He wrote:

The precipice was a grand study in black and white, its immense slabs shiny black with a thin veneer of ice, and decorated artistically with snow festoons and long slender icicle tassles. Verily the giant had donned his coat of mail, and meant to do his best to repel our attack; but his preparations where incomplete. A little more ice on the middle obstacle, a little further loosening of a splinter of rock at the top pitch, and we should have been driven back, unsuccessful. Maybe he thought us too wise to attempt the climb under such adverse conditions; but we were not and the mistake spelt his defeat.

We roped at the foot of the crags and I started up the left of the gully. The direct route could have been taken with greater ease, but a solid jet of ice cold water was shooting straight down the middle, and we preferred to stay dry a while longer. I mounted the wall from ledge to ledge, turning periodically at distances of four or five yards to manipulate the rope for the second man, who in his turn steadied the last man up. It is easier, not to say far more pleasurable, to climb than to describe the process.

Keeping up the wall for 60ft., we were then able to traverse along a narrow terrace into the gully, and the hard work began in earnest. Vertically upwards sprang the great cleft, with massive boulders many tons in weight, dividing it into separate storeys like the rungs of a gigantic ladder. On our heads dripped the water thawing from the upper rocks, uncomfortable at first, but preferable to the vagrant falling stones that haunt the locality in summer time. There was no drift of snow that might help us up the first few feet of each pitch. The side walls were clothed in wet ice. We wriggled up yard by yard, working closer together for mutual aid. So long as the gully remained narrow we were safe, for it was easy to hold in by leaning across from side to side.

Then came the first overhanging bit at the middle pitch, and while Field braced firmly in the innermost recesses, steadying the rope, the second man balanced himself astride the gully, outstanding on the slenderest of ledges. Then I clambered onto his shoulders to reach the outer edge of the roofing stone that overhung our course. Its upper surface was steeply sloping, and a jet of water plumping onto its centre radiated out a spray of liquid from which there was no escape. Sharp was the word, for strength and courage languish rapidly under such penetrating influences. But I could find nothing to hang onto, so smoothly lubricated did every hold seem, until an aperture was discovered in the roof through which a loop of rope could be passed from below. This served excellently, and I hastily drew myself up with its aid. The others followed with greater speed though they could not dodge the waterfall, and we stayed a moment to wring out our coats before continuing the assault.

If variety were charming, we had charmed lives. Up the next ladder we went, through one obstacle, over the next and 'chimneying' up between the third and the great wall, the leader using the shoulders and heads of his companions, their upstretched hands steadying his precarious footholds, and their expert advice supporting him all through. And with it all the most sublime views outwards and upwards and downwards of Nature's simple and severe architecture, designed and executed in her grandest style.

At last we came to the final obstacle, the limit of previous exploration. We had arrived at a little platform deep in the mountain, and three enormous boulders, one on top of the other, overhanging more and more near to the top, had to be circumvented. There was no way behind them; the only possibility was to work up one side wall and climb past them. I flung off my boots and Norfolk jacket, expecting to give the second man a bad time standing on his shoulders at the take-off, and attempted to climb up a narrow fissure in the left wall. Unhappily it proved to be useless, and we were all supremely uncomfortable when it was discovered I would have to descend again.

Next the right wall was tried and I blessed the previous three months' monotonous training with heavy dumbbells. The strain of the arms was excessive. Fortunately, there was no running water there, or the cold would have been unendurable. At the worst corner, by hanging on with the right hand and with the left looping part of my rope through the recess at the side of the boulder, a good grip was improvised. Of natural holds there was none of that smooth icy wall and the loop was a perfect boon. Even a perfect boon is hard to utilise when hands and toes are benumbed and all one's muscles are racked with prolonged tension. But the loop served its purpose, and after a few more struggles in the crack a ledge was reached from which it was evidently an easy scramble to the head of the gully.

"Réussi;-parfaitment-messieurs-send up my coat and boots!" The gasping message was finished in English to save delay, but I shiveringly waited many minutes in soft snow before the rope could be untied and the articles in question slung up on it. A cherished pair of socks fell out of the coat pocket as it was hauled over the edge of the top boulder, and took a preliminary clear drop of two or three hundred feet. It gave us quite a shock at the time for we thought it was a packet of sandwiches.

Then my companions came up, with an enviable surplus of warmth and energy. We raced up the steep snow and rock that remained above us, and did not halt till we had crossed the fell and descended to our starting point near the foot of Pillar Rock. There we sat in a protected corner, and I put my frozen feet into others' pockets, my dignity into my own, while we ate the crushed remnants of our lunch and discussed the day's excitements. When the grateful diffusion of animal heat had brought sensation to my extremities, and the spare energy of the whole party had spent itself in dragging on my boots, we started off again and made our way over the snow-covered fells down to Wasdale.

The route is now graded Severe (Hard) with a warning that the top pitch may be found very severe if the climber is short. To find a present-day climber tackling it, even with the tremendous advantage of modern equipment, under conditions similar to that prevailing on the first ascent, is unimaginable. In perfect conditions climbers have been known to fail on the last pitch. Some have remained there all night below the final chockstone and have had to be rescued the next day!

George Abraham wrote:

We were now at the foot of the formidable top pitch, which had never been climbed. A sudden seriousness settled on us all as we looked up at it, and remembered that this pitch had defied some of the finest cragsmen of our time. . . .

We were all suffering acutely from cold, especially Field, on account of his inaction, though he declared that the excitement of our movement kept him warm. Notwithstanding this, our leader, taking off his boots and jacket, prepared for a long struggle on that icy wall, whilst I padded my head to gain an inch or two in height. . . . The next few minutes were anxious ones; we shivered with cold, and held the rope firmly in case there should be a mishap higher up. Almost immediately there was a rush of falling snow, far out over the pitch, and it scarcely needed our leaders jodel of success to assure us that at last Walker's Gully had yielded to the onslaught of the climber. . . .

The situation was still rather serious, for we were perched on a narrow snow ledge on the very brink of the upper chock-stone; and the three of us were almost in a state of collapse from cold and the saturated state of our clothes. . . . The race up the steep snow seemed to revive our spirits, and, by the time the dry rocks below Great Doup were reached our suffering gave way to the glow of success. One little excitement was still in store for us, for Jones told us he was threatened with frostbite in both feet. On removing his boots we found that his statement was true, so we rubbed his feet with soft snow, and before putting on his boots, the troublesome feet were placed as far as possible in the pockets of the warmest member of the party, until circulation was thoroughly restored.

Night was drawing on apace, so we bade farewell to the 'vanquished foe', and were soon scampering along the High Level bound for the well earned comforts of Wasdale.

The following day Jones was out climbing! The same party, joined by J. W. F. Forbes, put up a new route on Overbeck above the Wasdale Valley. It was called 'E Chimney' (now known as Ash Tree Chimney) and is graded Very Difficult. Jones was never again to climb in the Lake District.

Easter and Whit had him visiting Wales and, typically, doing new climbs. The summer holidays arrived and he was off to the Alps. He was never to return.

It would seem that Jones's main ambitions lay in the Alps among the big mountains, and he wrote: "Of a truth many of our most prized little gems in Cumberland are but slightly better than boulder problems. Taken singly they cannot be reckoned for much Alpine practice, nor can our ability to surmount them justify us in assuming airs of superiority over many of general elementary experience abroad."

On Monday 28th August 1899 on the iced ridge of the Dent Blanche the leading guide fell. Attempting to surmount the Gendarme, which forms the last serious difficulty, Furrer (guide) stood on an ice-axe held by Zurbriggen (guide) and Jones. Reaching over the top, his hands gripped, then slipped. He pulled four men to their deaths. Zurbriggen and Jones went and Vuignier (guide) who was standing opposite. Fortunately the rope between Vuignier and Hill broke. They were swept to their deaths without uttering a sound. Hill alone remained, and his descent to the village in terrible conditions was a valiant and tenacious effort. He was on the go, without food, for over fifty hours.

Jones was buried at Evolena in the graveyard of a Roman Catholic church and in sight of the gleaming snows of the Dent Blanche.

George Abraham wrote,

Thus perished one of the most accomplished and fearless mountaineers of modern times. We had in solemn moments discussed the question of accidents, and I have no doubt that he died in the way he would himself have chosen. The end of O. G. Jones, the cheeriest of companions and most kindly of friends, was a pure accident, sudden and unexpected. How aptly has the poet sung of the voice of the mountain, the Dent Blanche might almost be speaking in the words,

> 'Crowned with the glory of the eternal snow,
> We hold high converse with the stars and sun,
> The little race of men how should we know,
> Or the low levels where the course is run.
> Yet sometimes come the footsteps of the brave,
> Who dare the perils of the icy steep,
> Joy, health or fame we give them—or a grave,
> The good we welcome but the best we keep.'

In spite of, or rather perhaps because of, his incredible record, a number of people have tried to dismiss Jones with harsh words. It is inevitable, being only human nature, that in any generation when one man rises above the rest, then certain people will try to knock him down. Alistair Crowley in his 'confessions' regurgitates a number of unsavoury comments about Jones and suggests him to be a dangerous incompetent.

It is true that Jones was not born with a great natural ability. Ability he unquestionably had, but greatness he earned by dedicated work. Unextinguishable enthusiasm and energy for climbing were his main virtues. When in London he trained hard with weights and gymnastic exercise. At the start of a climbing holiday he would be fitter and stronger than most of his companions were at the end of a week or more's climbing. One of his fellow teachers wrote in the *Westminster Gazette*:

> If ever a man bought an exhilarating atmosphere into a public school common room without violating any traditions worth maintaining that man was Owen Glynne Jones. He was the very idea of mens sana in corpore sano, and we all felt that in him we had a colleague bright, scholarly, manly and brave. After school hours it was refreshing to see him devising some new form of training both legs and arms for future conquests in the Alps, and older men, whilst wearily entering from their classrooms, smiled at his feats with chair or table.

He is recorded as climbing church towers in the city to keep in form, and he once partly ascended Cleopatra's Needle on the Embankment. Other feats included girdling a railway engine, steam naturally, using only the heads of the boiler rivets. Haskett-Smith said: "His muscular endurance enabled him to think quietly in places where the ordinary man would have to give undivided attention to the question of holding on or getting down again." George Abraham, his close friend, remarked upon his outstanding strength: "The secret of his almost unequalled success as a rock-climber was his abnormal finger-power, and an exceptional gift of balance on small foot-holds."

His antics at the Wasdale Head Hotel are deservedly famous, for they display all the properties of the true climbing spirit. They were essentially physically difficult and pleasantly, if somewhat rowdily, broke the rules of respectability. Oppenheimer wrote in his book *The Heart of Lakeland* of the gymnast Jones:

> Only the gymnast succeeds; he begins by sitting on the table despite the warning notice above him of a half crown fine for such an offence; he lets himself down gently, and, suddenly twisting round, he braces his legs firmly against the crossbars underneath; from above nothing can now be seen of him but one hand clutching the cushion, but all are watching down below to see that he does not touch the ground. After a struggle his other hand and his leg appear on the opposite side of the table leg, and a moment afterwards he is sitting breathless on the table once more, amidst loud cheers. Then the respective advantages of tall and short men in climbing are discussed, and the heights and reaches of all in the room are marked on the wall. Next the billiard room traverse is suggested, but no one responds. After much pressing the gymnast consents to try. He takes off his coat and shoes, and placing his hands on the edge of the billiard table he walks backwards up the wall to within a yard of the ceiling. Then he moves

along the table and wall simultaneously with hands and feet, avoiding the framed chromolithographs as well he may. With an enormous stride he reaches from one wall to another at the corner of the room, and is just saved from upsetting some half-emptied glasses of whisky on the mantelshelf by the terrified shouts of the owners. The next corner is easier, and in the middle of the third wall he can rest his legs awhile on the window ledge. The fourth wall is more difficult again; it contains a large recess, too deep to reach from the billiard table and only a foot lower than the ceiling. All round the angle of this he must pass before he arrives at the door, which is set diagonally across the corner of the room. This is the mauvais pas of the performance. The gymnast cautiously brings one foot down until his toe rests on the latch hold; then supporting himself from the corner of the billiard table with one hand he reaches the top of the door lintel with the other, lets go with the first, swings round in the opening and catches the lintel on the opposite side also. Here he gets the first rest for his arms by jamming himself tightly in the opening with his back and legs. To complete the traverse in the orthodox way he has still to work along the passage as far as the smoke room, and this, after an uncomfortable rest, he quickly does with back against one wall and feet against the other, finally opening the smoke room door and descending to terra firma. The tales and visions of the company there assembled are interrupted by cheers, and those who have missed the performance unreasonably clamour for a repetition. An old hand insidiously suggests that there are three variations of the move into the doorway, and the gymnast is dragged back once more to try them. Then there are tests of balance, of hanging on the rope and lifting people with it, or wriggling through narrow chair backs, and the evening wears away in attempting or watching all kinds of mad antics.

Probably the most amazing tale of them all was related by Abraham:

One Christmas time an ice axe was arranged as a horizontal bar, some marvellous feats were shown by experts, but Jones who had been watching retiring from the end of the room came forward and astonished everybody. He grasped the bar with three fingers of his left hand, lifted me with his right arm, and by sheer force of muscular strength raised his chin to the level of the bar three times.

Jones did not have good eyesight, and his sense of direction was poor. He frequently got lost. Haskett-Smith said:

Strangely different opinions have been held of this climber and there is an element of truth and falsehood in them all . . . condemned as unsportsmanlike, conceited and self-centred. The fact is that to bring out his best qualities he needed a good guide not to precede him but to follow him. Once shown the way he had enough strength and dexterity to deal with the minutiae of any climb but his eyesight served him poorly for distant detail. Self-centred he undoubtedly was, what was mistaken for conceit was his scientific determination to speak only of what he knew. He had studied his own physical powers as a chauffeur studies his car and for that reason he talked a good deal of himself.

The charge of being unsportsmanlike arose during his early visits to the Alps, when he was really unaware of the little canons and conventions of mountaineering.

Instances of his getting lost in Cumberland are many. He once, with a friend, set off for Windy Gap and Mosedale via the Stark Ridge of Yewbarrow and tramped for hours in poor visibility. Come evening they descended into what Jones thought was Wasdale; his companion commented: "Finally all doubt was at an end as we opened out the profile of the Angler's Rock in Ennerdale Water, cut sharp against the sunset."

Jones tells of a "photographic friend" who left his camera at the foot of Deep Ghyll while he intended to go quickly up Lord's Rake to Scafell Cairn and then down via Broad Stand (an hour's trip). The mist descended, and when night arrived he found himself in Boot village, many miles and many hours away from his camera. Still, quite a number of people make this mistake, myself included!

When Jones climbed, he invariably climbed hard and always with the intention of success. Once embarked on a particular course, his determination was absolute. Even so, Jones was not reckless, nor a fool. He weighed up the possibilities and then climbed accordingly. In extreme climbing, however, the balance is very fine, and he undoubtedly tipped the scales the wrong way on occasions.

One day he attempted to solo (that is, to climb alone) Moss Ghyll on Scafell, which at the time had a reputation for being one of the hardest routes. Winter conditions prevailed and the rocks were covered by a layer of soft snow. Reaching the Collie's Step successfully, he attempted to move out left from the great chockstone, and so to climb up that wall. The snow hid the step and any other holds that might have been of use.

He fell off but was fortunately held by a 'back-rope' which he had arranged in the cave underneath the chockstone. (A back rope is a system that a solo climber arranges to protect himself—it is supposedly a very modern technique.) Badly bruised and with two cracked ribs, he was lucky. If his system of belaying had failed or the hemp rope had broken, then he would have fallen four hundred feet to the broken rocks below. Jones picked himself up, climbed the pitch and finished the route.

In April 1898 he had returned to 'C' Gully on the screes to repeat his own climb. Some poor rock on which he was climbing broke away and he was again saved by the rope. When George Abraham arrived at the Wasdale Head Hotel, Jones was in bandages. He greeted George with the words, "Promise me you'll never climb 'C' Gully on the screes! It's a deadly place."

Iron Crag Gully one Christmas was the scene of Jones's over-enthusiasm. Iron Crag is situated along the continuation of the Thirlmere Valley. People looking at its impressive profile from the A591, Keswick to Ambleside road, often mistake it for Raven Crag. Some three hundred feet high, it stands on a major fault line, and the rock is rotten. Iron Crag Gully is a fundamentally unsafe climb and seems to have changed every time I visit the crag due to sections of it falling away.

The Abraham brothers, their father and Jones arrived at the climb late in the day. Water was pouring down it, and all except Jones thought it prudent to leave well alone. Of course he would not hear of leaving without at least attempting the gully. It took them many hours, and darkness was rapidly approaching when Jones emerged from the top.

During the ascent he had nearly killed the Abrahams when a complete ledge he was standing on fell away. It fortuitously missed the brothers, although George had the heel ripped from his boot, and hit the chimney wall just above their father. It shattered into a million pieces, being heavily jointed, and he was miraculously unhurt.

When the others got to the top, Jones had disappeared. They searched for an hour but could not find him. Their father asked: "Is he subject to fits?" When they eventually reached their home in Keswick, walking of course, they found Jones toasting his feet in front of the fire. George wrote:

So finished one of the most exciting days we ever spent with Owen Glynne Jones; and its events are indelibly stamped on my memory. But, full of incidents as the day had been, my pleasantest recollection is of the evening that followed; when, by the fire and over our pipes, we fought old battles over again, recalling to life happy days and exciting moments on the Fells, ending with the songs and hymns Jones loved so well to sing, and across the space of years, taking us back to the dear dead days, will come into our mind's eye the picture of him kneeling by the piano, singing with the keen enthusiasm which characterised every thing he did, his favourite hymn—

> Lead Kindly Light, amid the encircling gloom . . .
> O'er moor and fen, o'er crag and torrent,
> Till the night is gone.

Jones was undoubtedly a fanatic: his cure for frostbite was to put his fingers in boiling glue. In the Alps he permanently twisted some fingers out of shape using the 'remedy'. He also used to time his climbing and continually tried to improve his performance. Eventually he was able to climb the Kern Knotts Crack and descend Kern Knotts Chimney in a time of seven minutes. (Who said the Russians invented speed climbing?)

His book *Rock Climbing in the English Lake District* was first published in 1897. Beautifully illustrated with photographs by the Abraham brothers, it was a revelation and has been reprinted a number of times. Naturally it was the first real rock-climbing book, yet today, almost a hundred years later, it is difficult to imagine any improvement. One of its main contributions was the introduction of a scientific system of grading. This system, albeit somewhat expanded, is still used today. Jones wrote:

A rough classification is here appended of some sixty of the well known courses judged under good conditions. They are divided into four sets. The first are easy and adapted for beginners, the second set are moderately stiff, those of the third set rank as the difficult climbs of the district, and the last are of exceptional severity. Some attempt has been made to arrange them in their order of difficulty, the hardest ones coming last; but the variations of condition of each due to wind, temperature, rain, snow or ice are so extensive that no particular value should be attached to the sequence. But even if only approximately correct, the list may help men in deciding for themselves where to draw the line that shall limit their own unaided performances. As for the items in the fourth class, they are best left alone.

Mark the well-known words of an expert (Mr. C. Pilkington); 'The novice must on no account attempt them. He may console himself with the reflection that most of these fancy lists of rock-work are not mountaineering proper, and by remembering that those who first explored these routes, or rather created them, were not only brilliant rock gymnasts but experienced cragsmen.'

It should be noted that Jones was responsible for six of the nine Exceptionally Severe courses that were listed. His grades were Easy, Moderate, Difficult and Exceptionally Severe. Many of these routes are still graded as Jones first graded them.

The book gave a tremendous boost to the popularity of rock climbing. It is true to say that all subsequent rock-climbing development has been built on the foundation laid down by Jones. For in climbing, as in life, when information is collected and made freely available, people use it to their advantage. Climbers began to realize what was possible and what was not.

Somebody recently, a modern-day Extreme leader, asked me if I believed the story of Jones doing his one-arm pull-ups. How could anyone doubt it?

	Route name	Grade	Location
1892	East Pisgah Chimney		Pillar Rock
1893	Sergeant Crag Gully	HS	Langstrath
	Kern Knotts Chimney	D	Kern Knotts
1896	Jones's Route from Deep Ghyll	S	Scafell
1897	C Gully	MVS	The Screes
	Central Chimney	S	Dow Crag
	Kern Knotts West Chimney	D	Kern Knotts
	Kern Knotts Crack	MVS	Kern Knotts with H. C. Bowen
1898	Jones's Route Direct from Lord's Rake	S	Scafell
	Jones's Route	HVD	Dow Crag
	Jones and Collier's Climb	VD	Scafell
	Pisgah Buttress	VD	Scafell
	B Chimney Overbeck	D	
1899	Walker's Gully	HS	Pillar Rock
	E Chimney Overbeck	VD	

4

Frederick William Botterill
(d. 1920)

A decade ahead of his time, Yorkshireman Fred Botterill was a rock-climbing genius. He was a brilliant natural climber who, like many persons born with extreme talent, was seemingly devoid of ambition. Thoroughly modest, Fred never knew how good he was.

His ascent up the great slab of rock which daringly sweeps down the precipice of Scafell Crag, in 1903, was one of Lakeland's most dazzling climbing achievements. Although his contribution to Lakeland climbing was anything but prolific, his ascent of that slab, now known as Botterill's Slab, ensured him a place in climbing history.

Such was Fred's nature that one day he would climb the hardest routes of the time, effortlessly and in style, and the next he would go out of his way to lead a group of complete beginners up some obscure, easy climb, a route that would be no more than a walk to him. A greater contrast than this man with Jones is hard to imagine.

One factor that suggests that Fred's talent may not have been completely embryo when he commenced climbing among the Cumberland Fells is an important one. It has been responsible for shaping Lakeland climbing over successive generations. Born and brought up in Leeds, Fred from an early age had been scrambling and climbing about on his local gritstone outcrops.

Today gritstone climbing is reputed to offer the finest climbing training of all; indeed many 'gritstoners' postulate that there is no finer climbing. It is rough, round, pebbly and hard sedimentary rock. The climbs are invariably short and hard.

Because gritstone edges are generally short, although some reach a height of ninety feet, the climbing is relatively non-serious. Climbers can push themselves to their absolute gymnastic limit without the psychological problems (fear of falling off) that are present on Lake District climbs. To examine the list of climbers who have trained and developed on gritstone is to look at the *Who's Who* of the climbing world. Those who have subsequently taken their expertise to the Lakeland crags include Kelly, A. T. Hargreaves, Dolphin, Whillans, Brown, Austin, Livesey and many more.

Balance is learned on the steep-angled slabs which offer a high coefficient of friction and thus enable climbing where there are no holds as such. One merely 'pads' up them, keeping moving with the palms of the hands flat against the rock and taking short, smooth steps with the feet. To stop is to slide down to the bottom again, and to go too fast results in a foot slipping with the same result. In this way Fred Botterill must have developed his great technique.

It was Whitsun 1903 when Botterill and two companions, H. Williamson and J. E. Grant, found their way to the Wasdale Head. A number of days were spent climbing the ordinary routes. Then on 3rd June they investigated the Great Slab of Scafell. Botterill gave an account of the climb in the 1903 Yorkshire Ramblers' Club Journal. He starts the account with an interesting preamble: "The idea of a new climb of any importance in the Wasdale district had never crossed our minds, and the suggestion of one on Scafell Crags—perhaps the most frequented rocks of all—would, if proposed, have been received with derision." How many times has this been said since 1903? He continued the article with a graphic description of his subsequent ascent:

Clearing away the moss from little cracks here and there I managed to climb slowly upwards for about 60 feet. The holds then dwindled down to little more than finger-end cracks. I looked about me and saw, some 12 feet higher, a little nest about a foot square covered with dried grass. Eight feet higher still was another nest and a traverse leading back to where the crack opened into a respectable chimney. If I could only reach hold of that first nest what remained would be comparatively easy. It seemed to be a more difficult thing than I had ever done but I was anxious to tackle it. Not wishing to part with the axe I seized it betweeen my teeth and with my fingers in the best available cracks I advanced. I cannot tell with certainty how many holds there were; but I distinctly remember that when within two feet of the nest I had a good hold with my right hand on the face, and so ventured with my left to tear away the dried grass on the nest. However, the grass removed from the ledge, a nice little resting place was exposed, painfully small, but level and quite safe. I scrambled onto it, but on account of the weight of the rope behind me, it was only with great care and some difficulty that I was able to turn round. At last I could sit down on the nest and look around me.

The view was glorious. I could see Scafell Pike and a party round the cairn. Far below was another group intent on watching our movements, a lady being amongst the party. I once read in a book on etiquette that a gentleman in whatever situation of life should never forget his manners towards the other sex, so I raised my hat, though I wonder if the author had ever dreamed of a situation like mine. I now discovered that our 80 feet of rope had quite run-out and that my companions had already attached an additional 60 feet. Further, I began to wonder what had become of my axe and concluded I must unthinkingly have placed it somewhere lower down. There it was, stuck in a little crack about five feet below me. Not knowing what was yet to come I felt I must recover it, so I lowered myself until I could reach it with my foot. I succeeded in balancing it on my boot, but in bringing it up it slipped and clattering on the rocks for a few feet took a final leap and stuck point downwards in the Rake's Progress. Standing up again I recommenced the ascent and climbed on the second nest à cheval, from where, after a brief rest, I began to traverse back to the crack. This was sensational but perfectly safe. As usual I started with the wrong foot, and after taking two steps was obliged to go back. The next time I started with the left foot, then came the right, again the left, and lastly a long stride with the right, brought me into the chimney. The performance was what might have been called a pas de quatre. Complimentary sounds came from my companions below, but without stopping to acknowledge these I pulled myself up ten feet higher onto a good grass covered ledge to the right of the crack, smaller but very similar to the Tennis Court Ledge of Moss Ghyll.

Botterill's writing is factual and amusing, but to those who know the climb it shows the brilliance of the man. Quite simply this was the longest, hardest and most serious pitch that had ever been climbed in Britain. He had run out 120 feet of rope without any form of protection, and the climbing was of a standard hitherto unattained. The sweep of slab is completely open and exposed; nowhere on the pitch was there anything underneath him but space and the screes far below.

Some years previously the "only genuine Jones" had attempted the line and retreated, beaten by iced rocks. For him to be turned back, even due to adverse conditions, was so rare an event as to be unique.

A thoroughly modern climb, it consolidated Jones's attack on the Pinnacle Face (of Scafell) and markedly left the confining walls of the chimney and gully. A whole bold new era had been opened up. What a picture is conjured up by imagining Botterill climbing the pitch in bendy nailed boots (he did not even resort to socks) with rucksack and ice-axe. He had not inspected the pitch from above by use of the rope, and the way up to Virgin Slabs was unknown. He had not only to select the route as he climbed but also to remove the grass and loose rock.

I think his account shows well that he was totally oblivious of the mental barrier; indeed, he did not seem to be at all pressed by the technical difficulty. As for sitting down in the middle of that smooth two-hundred-foot sweep of exposed slab, and taking his hat off to the lady below, he was not only a perfect gentleman but also a rock-climbing genius. I often wonder by how many feet his falling ice-axe missed the awestruck audience standing on the Rake's Progress far below.

Botterill continued:

'How is it now?' my companions inquired. 'Excellent,' I replied, 'a good belaying pin and just room for three. Do you feel like following?' Without answering me the second man commenced the traverse to the chimney edge whilst I carefully belayed the rope. Up he came in splendid style and without stopping, taking only a quarter of the time it had taken me. He then untied and we threw down the 140 feet of rope to our third who soon joined us. We hailed a climbing friend who was watching from the Progress and invited him to join us, but he very generously refused and said he would hover near lest we might not be able to advance further and require the aid of a rope from above.

We next christened our berth 'Coffin Lodge', built a cairn on it and left our names on a card. Starting off again a long stride with the left foot took the leader back into the crack, and a stiff climb of 20 to 30 feet landed us all into an extraordinary chimney, which though only wide enough to comfortably admit the body sideways ran right into the crag for about 15 feet. Like the crack below it leaned to the left at an angle of 70 degrees or so. About 25 feet up a chockstone and debris formed a roof and suspended in the middle some six feet below it, were three more chockstones. When the second man had joined me he exclaimed with astonishment: 'What a place. How can we get out?' 'Wait a bit,' I answered, although I could not then see a way. However, I went as far as I could into the crack and with restricted use of back and knee climbed upwards until the level of the suspended chockstones was reached; from there a narrow ledge rendered these easily accessible. They were securely wedged and safe to stand upon. The ledge continued along out of the crack until the most outward chockstone of the roof was within reach. This I seized with both hands, and a steady pull upwards landed me into the Puttrell Chimney of Keswick Brothers' Climb.

Hence the climb was successfully accomplished. Out of step with the rest of climbing development, it remained unattempted and unrepeated for nine years—indeed, until the next 'climbing generation' arrived. Ernest A. Baker, who climbed with Botterill, wrote in his book *The British Highlands with Rope and Rucksack*, when talking of the bleak climbing years after Jones's death: "There was one exception in the achievements of that brilliant young athlete Fred Botterill, whose fine balance and sense of touch enabled him to lead up perilous slabs by minute finger holds, where nobody for years was anxious to follow."

The terrible accident on Jones's Route Direct on Scafell Pinnacle in September 1903 stifled all further development for a number of years. It was not until 8th June 1906 that Botterill was to pioneer another new route.

North West Climb (MVS) on Pillar Rock is hard and quality climbing. It gives four hundred feet of good rock, and the situations are superb. The standard is maintained throughout, and it reaches a crescendo near the top, where it is both difficult and exposed. Of course it was led by Fred, but the party included his brother Arthur, who was a gymnast, J. H. Taylor and L. J. Oppenheimer who published, in 1909, a most charming book called *The Heart of Lakeland*. The eighth pitch of the route was named Taylor's Chimney, though nowadays Lamb's Chimney to the right is taken, and the tenth pitch Oppenheimer's Chimney. Presumably, Botterill was too modest to put his name to any individual section of the climb although he led the entire route. George Abraham wrote in his book *The Complete Mountaineer*:

> The success of a party led by Mr. F. W. Botterill up the north-west side of the famous rock in 1906 demands attention as a remarkable performance, but the route is much too difficult to become either useful or popular. This and the direct ascent of Scafell Pinnacle should be classed as sui generis. They are not justifiable, without careful exploration and preparation. The latter might well include a strong gymnasium net fixed below the steepest portion.

His next route, done the following year, lay in Buttermere. It was the first climb done on Haystacks, a great heap of loose rock and vegetation above Warnscale Bottom, and it has an evil reputation. The grade is Severe and the Fell and Rock Climbing Club guidebook says: ". . . it is a climb which should be left severely alone owing to the loose and rotten rocks".

The same year Crescent Climb in Langdale was done. It is graded Moderate and is a very easy climb. Even so, in my opinion it is one of the best natural lines on Pavey Ark. It looks much harder than it actually is, and its main feature, from below, is a seemingly delicate traverse under a great crescent-shaped overhang of rock. When arriving at the traverse, and only then, it can be seen that a horse and cart could be driven across in 'complete safety'. Combined with Gwynne's Chimney (D) above (this is how Botterill climbed it), it makes one of the best courses of that standard in the Lakes.

A handful of rather pleasant new routes was done in 1909. During this time Fred had decided to take almost a full year off and live in his 'gypsy' caravan 'The Bertol' based at Wasdale Head. To get it there, he put it on the train at Leeds and had a team of heavy horses pull it to Wasdale. Imagine Botterill, puffing his pipe, being pulled along beneath the Lakeland Fells by a pair of mighty Clydesdales, their feathered hooves gently tapping the unmetalled road. Feel the thrill of excitement knowing that the summer is yours to do with as you please. Picture also Wasdale Head in 1909: no crowds, no campers, no noise, no nuclear power stations billowing out clouds of steam stolen from Wastwater, just the peace and serenity of the fells and the natural friendliness of the local Cumbrians.

It was a magical summer for the city dweller and rock climber. Botterill wrote an account which captures this bygone age and shows his deep love and appreciation of his situation. A timeless article, it fills one unashamedly with envy:

THE LOG OF BERTOL

'The Bertol' is the name of our caravan. As private vans go it is small; for a gipsy van it is large. In it is centred, for use, all that goes to make what we call 'home'. It has become the focus of our lives. If we are overtaken by storm, feel wet and cold, or lose our way, our thoughts spontaneously turn to the Bertol and its pleasant interior as a panacea for our discomfort. . . .

The discomforts of the 'Bertol' life may be counted on the fingers of one hand. It would require many hands to count the discomforts of the 'high-wall' home, with its limited sky, its lack of sun, air, and light, its dust, its cleanings—that labour of Sisyphus—its frozen pipes, its gas-polluted air, its coughs and colds. . . .

Much might be said of the preliminaries, but let us break in at Drigg Station, and putting back the Bertol on to its wheels, see it slowly dragged by two powerful horses up to Wasdale Head, and fixed in its quarters, near the Schoolhouse and facing the Lake; There to commence our summer life in real earnest on the morrow.

March 22–27: These days have been spent alternating between climbing and work at home. We have painted the outside, and re-upholstered our camp chairs. We have made a footstool and sewed an awning for the front. We have climbed Central Gully in Great End (in ice), and vanquished the Needle Ridge. We have spent two days in Moss Ghyll, being beaten on the first day by the traverse from Tennis Court Ledge. We have failed to do Piers Ghyll in spite of 25 feet of snow, a bergschrund at the Great Pitch being too much for us. We have seen tons of ice and rock fall spontaneously from Gable Crag. The working days have been as enjoyable as the climbing, and stand out in our memories. We have had a pride in our work and the shade from the awning seems a better shade, or, shall we say, a shade better, because it is of our own handicraft. It begins to dawn

Scafell, a cliff which, more than any other, monitors the development of early rock climbing. From left to right: Botterill's Slab (VS, 1903); Central Buttress (HVS, 1914); Moss Ghyll Grooves (MVS, 1926); Jones's Route on the Pinnacle Face (S, 1898).

Knife-Edge Arete, Scafell, climbed by Haskett-Smith in 1888.

(*above*) W. P. Haskett-Smith (1915) —
'The Father of Rock Climbing'.

(*left*) J. W. Robinson, who provided
both W. P. Haskett-Smith and
O. G. Jones with local knowledge.

(*opposite*) The famous Napes Needle, first climbed (solo) by W. P.
Haskett-Smith in 1886.

O. G. Jones — 'the only genuine
Jones'.

Fred Botterill, a rock-climbing genius.

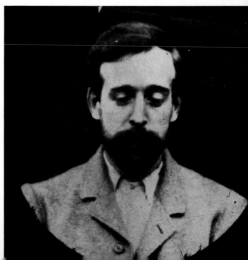

'The Bertol' and Fred Botterill at Wasdale Head.

(opposite top)   The top of Jones's Arete, Scafell Pinnacle — the ground lies 400 feet below. It was first climbed by Jones in 1898.

(opposite bottom)   The incredibly precarious and exposed Botterill's Slab (VS) on Scafell, first climbed by Fred Botterill in 1903.

S. W. Herford on the great Central Buttress of Scafell, 1914.

(*top* S. W. Herford
left) led on the W
ern Front bu
spirit still re
the hills'

(*above*) H. M. Ke

H. M. Kelly on t
Scoop Cast
Naize (gritston
demonstrating h
technique in 'ru
bers'.

Emily Kelly, a s
perb balance clir
ber.

Scafell Crag. The climbers are on H. M. Kelly's superb Moss Ghyll Grooves (MVS, 1926). On their left in the centre of the wall can be seen the crack of the great flake on Central Buttress, first climbed by S. W. Herford (and G. S. Sansom) in 1914 and graded Hard Very Severe today.

Tophet Wall on the Napes, Great Gable, first climbed by H. M. Kelly in 1923.

upon us that one great joy in life is the joy of making things for oneself. . . .

March 28: We are awakened somewhat abruptly this morning to the fact that another Rambler has arrived. The van shakes terribly and there is a violent kicking at the panels. The noise comes from outside and may best be explained by the following entry in the log: It is here at last—The Caravan Traverse! After a week spent in reposeful peace it came upon us this morning like a bolt from the blue(s). 'The great difficulty is avoiding the owner of the van. The start, which is not easy, consists in getting out unobserved. An alternative route is to take the can and say you are going for water. If this 'Can Route' is taken the can must first be filled. This will no doubt deter most parties from attempting it. During the first heavy rain after the traverse was accomplished, the roof of the van, after ten minutes, leaked in two places. The owner says if the traverse is attempted again the party may as well take the whole 'darned' roof home to practise on. Only a rope's end was used. The climb is likely to become more difficult as the owner is about to place spikes on the handholds. If, as is threatened, the owner uses his revolver, it will become an exceptionally severe course.' . . .

Another day is spent in the Wood, ascending by one tree and descending by another—an old-fashioned feat. Another is trying a new buttress on the Napes. The weather is clearing and we are having one of life's greatest joys—meals in the open. We sit out in our pyjamas and eat our breakfast in the grateful warmth of the sun. How beautiful Gable looks—and the lake shimmering in the heat—Yewbarrow with a hundred hues—Burnmoor a mysterious beyond, in the dazzling sun—the Pillar deep purple—the sky brilliant green! There is too much to look at—our brain whirls with an excess of delight and shutting our eyes we settle down in our chairs slumberously. Oh, the charm of it all! Our cup of happiness is full to the brim! To speak would break the spell.

April 7: We make the first ascent of the Abbey Ridge. . . . The rocks are crowded and we meet many old friends on the climbs. How pleasant it is to meet them! . . .

April 25–26: But simple recollections remain to us of these days. We have been to tea in the Wood and the woodsman has told us strange tales of living on sevenpence per day. We develop photographs until far into the night and retire thankfully into our comfortable bunk. The wind rocks us gently and the Bertol becomes a cradle, the pitter-patter of the rain a lullaby, and we sleep long, deep, dreamless sleeps. . . .

April 27–May 4: Many climbers come and pass short holidays, and many a grand old cliff echoes our voices and rings with the clink of our nailed boots. We have but one grief. No sooner do we make friends than they are called away again to civilization. The Hounds are with us, lambs arrive in great numbers, the trees are in bloom and life is active everywhere. We are back in winter. The snow, which has been slowly disappearing, now falls heavily; the rocks are cold and icy, and our ice-axes are requisitioned. Eight busy days are spent with two doughty Alpine men. One of them, in the district for the first time, is insatiable, doing three and four climbs in the day. We tell G. we are exhausted and suggest we should accompany him on alternate days and so tire him out. On the day before he leaves we do six climbs, but with no such result, and we learn with joy that he afterwards fell into the sea, a victim to nailed boots and Seascale's mossy pier.

May 5–7: The winds are now supreme and our tent is blown down; one night we turn out and rope the van to the nearest trees. The gusts from the north are terrible; one of them lifts up the back of the Bertol; another blows a hen clean away; another takes the photographic prints, as they are drying, out of the van and round and up by the Schoolhouse; another snatches up the morning paper, opens a port, whips it through and closes down the port tight again. Such are the pranks it plays. The gusts are followed by dead calms. It is a fine sight to watch the wind sweep over the grass, shake the trees, and lash the Lake to a white foam.

We spy two men coming up the road on a tandem bicycle, and, in reply to a familiar call, rush out to find J. H. B. approaching—the other man is his rucksack. . . .

May 8–14: Happy days with meals in the open! Days on the Pillar, building cairns and marking paths, and tea on the summit. . . .

May 15–25: The dale is fox-ridden and farmers encircle their farms at night with lighted lamps. From one farm alone thirty-one lambs are lost. The glorious weather continues, and May wins the annual prize for the finest month. The Northern Lights appear and one night seven streamers are seen over the Pillar. . . .

One cloudy day on Lingmell we see the Brocken Spectre, an awe-inspiring sight. The sun is setting over Stirrup Crag and the mist floats in masses over the face of Scafell; from the crags of Lingmell, as we gaze into the depths of Piers Ghyll, D. excitedly calls our attention to a perfect oval rainbow, and in the midst of it are two shadows. We wave our arms and the spectre does the same, and as D. makes for his camera with outstretched arms, the spectre looks exactly like a cross. We are not surprised that, in tragic moments peasants have judged it a supernatural sign. The spectre fades and disappears, the glories of the sunset increase, Scotland and the Isle of

Man catch its colouring and with reluctance we descend in the gathering darkness.

The days pass swiftly on, each leaving its stamp on us and subtly changing our outlook upon life. When our thoughts turn to the city of bricks and mortar we have left, it seems like a maze, and we on one of its walls, wondering why the people fail to find a way out. . . .

June: A month of visitors, of suppers, of tea parties in the tent, of long walks and of exploration on the rocks. . . .

We make a new exit from Moss Ghyll, thirty feet to the right of Collier's Exit. It is difficult, but in winter when the Chimney is full of ice, it may be a feasible way. After an ascent of Walker's Gully, we keep to the rocks and climb to the summit of the Shamrock by its N.W. face. One perfect day we make a second attempt on the Engineer's Chimney on Gable Crag, and are again repulsed, unable, beyond a certain point, to make the slightest advance, and we doubt if it be the place to give a shoulder. A girdle traverse of the Needle from shoulder to shoulder, without touching the top, is a curious variation of the ordinary ascent.

July 1–31: The weeks become months and the summer slips away. People ask us if we do not tire of the mountains and if holidays do not pall. We smile as we think of our active existence and tell them that as yet we have only touched the fringe of our life in the mountains, for we are in a busy world and live busy lives. . . .

We have books with us, but they lie unopened, for the pink summit of Gable is above us, set in a framework of trees, and the scent of the firs, the songs of birds, the buzz of insects all around. A something enters our souls; we are reading the Book of Life.

August: Each day we probe a little further into the primitive, and each day impresses us more with our ignorance of our surroundings. . . .

September: We have given up climbing, for the time being, and have taken to gathering nuts and berries. . . .

December: And now as we write, the winter is upon us and all these things are past and gone. We have had a peep into a wonderful world and it seems as if the edge of a curtain had been lifted and dropped again. It is said to have been a wet year; to us it has been unprecedented sunshine. We begin to forget our little sadnesses and only the joys remain. No gay songs of birds greet us in the morning now, the days are dull and lifeless and the wind howls mournfully around, but the Bertol has no spare-room for sadness and we look forward hopefully to the future.

The final few lines lightly veil a tragedy that deeply affected Fred Botterill to the extent that he climbed but little again. C. E.

Bedford wrote: "Indeed almost too kind, where a weak party was in need of a leader, Fred would go miles out of his way to take up a course which to him was a simple walk, he was just as happy, just as keen on the sport in an easy gully as on an exceptionally severe face."

This was significant, for in September 1909 Botterill agreed to hold the rope for Thomas James Rennison. The latter was very keen to lead Eagle's Nest Ridge Direct (MVS) on the Napes face of Great Gable. This is a difficult climb and a serious lead, following the bold arete on the left of the Dress Circle (an area just behind the famous Napes Needle). Poorly protected with sloping holds, it was first led by G. A. Solly on a cold April day in 1892. It was the earliest climb to be classed as an Exceptionally Severe course by Jones. Despite its rather fearsome reputation, Botterill had ascended the climb on a number of occasions, and it lay well within his ability. He offered to climb as second man to Rennison merely as a gentlemanly act. (To climb second is to hold the rope and belay the lead climber.)

They had reached the belay ledge fifty feet above the Dress Circle, and Botterill was tied on paying out the rope to Rennison. Rennison was up on the arete way above Botterill making steady progress when he paused, then without warning silently fell. It was a long fall, and Botterill crouched on the ledge to take the strain. He was running the rope round a knob of rock to act as a slight friction break. As the force of the fall came on Botterill, he held the rope tightly, which was an act of great courage, but the rope parted round that knob of rock, and Rennison fell to his death. Botterill had done everything in his power to halt the fall; his only mistake lay in imagining that others had ability comparable to his own. Shattered, he never climbed seriously again.

George Sansom of Central Buttress fame said: "Botterill was unambitious; he was a very beautiful climber and could have done as much as Herford, or later Kelly, had he tried." For Sansom to compare any man with his great friend Siegfried Herford was a measure of the outstanding ability of Botterill.

Fred had, inborn, something which many climbers never have. It is best described as 'style'. Many men reach the top of the same climb, but the difference between an ordinary or even a poor ascent and an impressive display of climbing is that thing called style. He climbed with speed and certainty, rarely hesitating, and was a good climber to watch. Haskett-Smith wrote: "I never had a climb with him, though I often saw him climbing, brilliantly with the Seatrees. He was fond of taking a caravan among the Alps and invented an ingenious route up a difficult pinnacle on the Petit Dent de Veisivi."

Fred's adventure activities were reasonably diverse. Not only did he appreciate the natural open beauty of the Lake District Fells but he was an active pot-holer in his native Yorkshire. He also used to take part in an athletic game called 'Scouts and Outposts'. Basically a group of people would guard some part of the fells, a summit or tarn, and the Scouts would try to get there unobserved. It involves map-reading and orienteering skills and has to be accomplished within certain time limits.

Kindly natured, Fred always had a warm sense of humour. Once he announced at the Wasdale Head Hotel that he had made a record ascent of the Napes Needle.

"What time?"—"Half an hour!"

"Half an hour—that's no record."

"From the Hotel," concluded Fred. (Usually it takes a party, walking normally, 1½ hours just to reach the foot of the Needle, let alone climb it.)

As it was for Fred Botterill in climbing, so it was in life. During the holocaust of the First World War he joined up as a private. Later, he was made sergeant. He could not understand this and asked a climbing friend and officer what was the reason for this promotion. It did not occur to Fred that it could be anything to do with his personal ability. Offered a commission, he turned it down! During the War he contracted TNT poisoning, and this was officially to cause his death in 1920.

Really Fred Botterill climbed only for the fun of it, yet his impact on the climbing scene was immense. His greatest climb, that magnificent sweep of rock on Scafell, is aptly named Botterill's Slab.

Route name	Grade	Location	Comments
1903 Botterill's Slab	VS	Scafell	
1906 North West Climb	MVS	Pillar Rock	
1907 Warn Ghyll	S	Haystacks	
1907 Crescent Climb	M	Pavey Ark	
1909 North East Arete	D	Pillar Rock	
1909 Shamrock Buttress	VD	Pillar Rock	H. B. Gibson led

	Route name	*Grade*	*Location*	*Comments*
1909	Pisgah West Ridge (ordinary route and variation)	HVD	Pillar Rock	
1909	Abbey Buttress	VD	The Napes— Great Gable	
1919	Botterill's Exit to Moss Ghyll			

5

Siegfried Wedgwood Herford

(29th July 1891–1916)

Fred Botterill had been a man out of time, a wayward genius whom climbers of his generation could not comprehend. By the end of the first decade of the twentieth century a new breed of climber had begun to emerge. The most brilliant of this short-lived generation was Siegfried Wedgwood Herford.

His ascent of the renowned Central Buttress (HVS) on Scafell was one of the greatest Lakeland leads. Today climbers can be seen queuing to do this route. It remains, however, hard, and more climbers fail, or indeed fall off, the great flake than any other Lakeland climb. Herford's ascent of Central Buttress in 1914 is now popularly known as "probably the biggest single breakthrough in standard in the history of Lakeland climbing". But tragically this was a lost generation, for in 1914 the First World War began and stifled all further development.

Born on 29th July 1891, in Aberystwyth, Siegfried Wedgwood Herford was the son of gifted parents. He soon reflected their talents and entered the Engineering School of Manchester

University in 1909. Graduating in 1912, he was at the head of the honours list, winning a research scholarship. During the years 1913–14 he was employed at the Royal Aircraft Factory at Farnborough on aerial engineering problems.

His first climbing experiences came in 1907 when, at the age of sixteen, he took part in a number of ascents of the minor peaks in the Gross Glockner group. From 1909 to 1910 he undertook a limited amount of rock climbing in both England and Wales, his first major climb being the Great Gully on Craig-Yr-Ysfa. But, it was Easter 1911 when rock climbing began to be something very special in his life. Camping at Ogwen, he had a marvellous holiday and climbed on Glyder Fach, Crai-Yr-Ysfa, Glyder Fawr and Lliewedd, ticking off the hardest routes of that era.

From that moment he unashamedly spent all his spare time climbing. But 1912 was his first great year. J. Laycock, a notable gritstone expert recorded the fact that he and Herford climbed a hundred days of that year while both were working full time. Holidays in the Lakes and Wales became "fast and frequent".

The year commenced with a visit to the Dolomites where, accompanied by George S. Sansom, he ascended, guideless, Winkler and Stalder Thurm and H. Fanffinger Spitze. From Herford's writings it is obvious, however, that it was the modest but talented Sansom who was doing the leading on the Schmitt-kamin. Back in Britain they spent two weeks among the Cuillins on the Isle of Skye.

When they returned to the Lakes in April, the effects were devastating. They shattered the myth that the Pinnacle Face of Scafell was impregnable and promptly repeated Jones's route. This was the second ascent and was the first attempt since the terrible accident in 1903. They climbed the route in stockinged feet—realizing that the boots of their day were too clumsy for this delicate and serious face climb.

Sansom and Herford were seemingly inseparable friends. They were of like background; both loved the Lake District, and they were both superb climbers. They literally invaded Scafell, blowing to the wind the misgivings and fears of their predecessors, repeating not only Jones's Route on the Pinnacle Face but also the more exacting and precarious Botterill's Slab. They experienced no great difficulty, even though Jones's route had remained unrepeated for thirteen years and Botterill's Slab for nine years. The psychological barrier had been bridged by these two, climbers in their prime, brilliant, perfectly matched and unstoppable. The whole climbing world seemingly lay at their feet.

That year on Scafell they proceeded to make three new routes. One, the girdle traverse, planned by Sansom, was an original concept in Lakeland climbing. It is true that Herford had already girdled the Castle Naize, a Peak District gritstone crag that became the training ground for other great pioneers, but to traverse horizontally over such a large and formidable area of the rock that is the face of Scafell was something original and very daring. As for the other routes, they romped across the face of the Scafell Pinnacle, revelling in the extreme exposure and delicate nature of the climbing.

In describing these routes and exploits in an article entitled 'A Guide to the Scafell Pinnacle', they realized that they were opening up the face to climbers with, most probably, much less ability than themselves. With the existing safety techniques, or lack of them, they were very conscious of the potential dangers. So, with the accident of 1903 in mind, they wrote the following clarification:

> It is only after the most careful consideration that we have decided to describe the climbs. Hitherto, mention of them has been made chiefly in order to warn climbers to keep off them. We feel, therefore, that some justification is necessary for such a marked departure from precedent. In the first place, we do not think that sufficient distinction has been made, between difficulty and danger in climbing. In the case of a climb lying on a perfectly clean and sound rock, the apparent difficulty varies inversely as the skill of the individual, although the intrinsic or technical difficulty is, of course, the same for all. It is when the skill begins to be taxed to near its limit that danger is present. The danger, therefore, depends on the skill of the individual and can be eliminated if the skill is sufficiently great. The climb in itself is not dangerous. Suppose, however, the climb is upon rotten rocks. There the danger lies in the climb. No amount of skill can afford perfect security. It is these places which, in our opinion, should be avoided. In the former category come the climbs of the Pinnacle Face. We see no reason why the climbs on the Pinnacle Face should be regarded as intrinsically dangerous, but at the same time we would emphatically urge that they be not attempted by any but the steadfast and most skilful of leaders who, moreover, have had considerable

experience of difficult slab climbing without boots. We would most strongly emphasize the point that 'boots should be taken off'; the holds are so sloping in places (up to 40°) as to render climbing in boots excessively dangerous. These climbs are undeniably best tackled alone.

Probably their most technically difficult route of that incredible year, 1912, was an ascent that went almost unnoticed after their exploits on Scafell. This was the ascent of Kern Knotts West Buttress, Very Severe, on Great Gable. The climb was led by G. S. Sansom.

S. W. Herford, climbing extensively, was soon ascending all established routes. Amazingly, it was popularly believed, and how many times has this been repeated by each successive generation, that, "From 1911 it was no easy matter to discover good new climbs in England and Wales." To counter this he began to reverse routes and found that descending was quite different from ascending a route. He had invented an important variation to the sport. This was taken further by other, later great Lakeland pioneers, particularly H. M. Kelly, who always climbed down a route rather than make an easy descent following a path, and R. J. Birkett, who reversed the hard routes of his day wearing nailed boots.

Herford took this variation seriously enough to write an article entitled 'The Doctrine of Descent'. The following extract shows his perception and its challenge:

I come now to the free and open climbing of slabs and aretes, grooves and corners, mantel shelves and noses—in short, the higher forms of the sport. The essence of the whole matter is conveyed in one word—balance. . . . Is a finer sense of balance required in going down than in going up? In certain instances, I think it undoubtedly is. Take, for example, the case of a sloping slab with flat shelving holds on which exact footwork is essential. It is, to start with, much harder to gauge the value of a ledge below one's feet than above it—an important point when the hold slopes. . . .

The exceptionally high standard of English rock climbs develops a style of its own; a style, it is true, remarkable for its exactness, soundness and general deliberation, but which, if applied to this comparatively easy downhill work, is singularly ineffective.

Sansom and Herford had become the most formidable climbing partnership in Britain. George Sansom wrote in his article

'Goodbye to All That', when he was eighty-seven:

I had by this time an intense love for Wasdale and the fells around it. The delightful view of it from Napes Ridge often came to memory during the long war years, and I longed to see it again. As the poet expressed it: 'There are no hills like the Wasdale hills when Spring comes up the dale'. So great was my love for Wasdale that I had little wish to visit other regions, although my friends enthused about Skye, Scotland and Wales. I did climb in Wales for a few days but strangely enough I cannot recall a single day's climbing there that I really enjoyed. For some reason, which I do not understand, the Wasdale mountains seemed friendly, whilst the Welsh ones seemed hostile. Fortunately, Herford also preferred Wasdale, and we had many holidays together; we were both undergraduates; he was in engineering and I was in biology, so were usually able to get away together at New Year, Easter and Summer vacations. . . .

It was J. Laycock the gritstone expert, who first introduced me to Herford. We soon became friends; friendship which lasted until his death in the war. I do not think we ever had a quarrel or serious disagreement, and I felt his loss greatly. He was tall, slim and graceful in movement like Kipling's description of Kamal's son—'That dropped from a mountain crest. He trod the ling like a buck in Spring and looked like a lance in rest'. Herford was a most generous climber. He was much better than me yet he always offered me the lead; he also gave me credit for new climbs which in fact I had only planned, and he had led. I remember after we did the Girdle Traverse of Scafell, H. B. Gibson was writing up the account of it in the Wasdale book and he rightly put Herford's name first. Herford protested and said, 'Sansom planned the whole thing; he ought to come first'. But I supported Gibson; at that time I would not have tried to lead Botterill's Slab. Perhaps I was better at planning new routes, but Herford was the bolder climber. He was essentially a very safe leader and I never felt any anxiety when he was climbing.

Scafell Pinnacle Face had always attracted me and one day I got a friend to hold my rope at the Crevasse, while I explored it. I gradually worked my way down and across the slab to the foot of Lord's Rake. I found the rocks far less difficult than I expected, and the climbing very enjoyable, so I felt surprised that no-one seemed to have tried it since the accident to Broadrick's party in 1903. When I asked Botterill if he had ever tried it he said that the rocks were unsuitable for climbing; but it is possible that he tried in nailed boots, which are not advisable on the very sloping holds.

Herford and I thought the Pinnacle Face delightful. I remember, one wet day on the Pinnacle Face, Herford said 'You would be safer than me leading the Mantelshelf pitch, on these wet rocks'—and as a matter of fact a tall man does find that pitch very hard, whereas with my short height, it goes quite easily. A man once asked me how I did it so easily and I said: 'Imagine there is a foothold on the wall two feet up, step up on it with your right foot and put your left knee on the mantelshelf.' It sounds rather absurd to tell a man to step up on an imaginary hold, but that is what one actually does, the weight being taken by downward pressure of the hands.

It was also in 1912 that Herford and Sansom first spied the incredibly impressive line of Central Buttress. Climbing up and out of Moss Ghyll, following a grassy scoop, they were able to look leftwards and pick out the unbroken and vertical cliff opposite the great flake crack. Herford was convinced that there was a possibility of climbing this central portion of rock, although Sansom thought it impossible. Herford started a campaign that was to last until the successful ascent in 1914. His confidence and determination to return to this frightening and oppressive piece of rock, some three hundred feet high, was pure inspiration. No modern climber, some seventy years later, can fail to be impressed and more than a little intimidated by this super route.

The story is told by Sansom in his article 'Scafell Central Buttress':

Some two years ago, Herford and I, in an inquisitive spirit, climbed up a grassy scoop leading out of Moss Ghyll onto the Central Buttress. We did not seriously believe that we should find a new climb on this rock face, for it appears to be singularly unbroken and almost vertical for over two hundred feet. It was, however, an unknown region, and as such appealed to us.

The scoop was not very difficult and we were soon looking around a corner at the top along the narrow grassy ledge which apparently extended right across the face to Botterill's Slab. The rocks fell away very steeply below and a sheer smooth wall rose up to a great height above; its regularity was interrupted at one point, it is true, by an enormous rock flake which tapered out to nothing 70 feet higher. For some obscure reason this ledge suggested vague possibilities, which we did not fully appreciate at the time. The Great Flake looked quite hopeless as a means of ascent and we dismissed the idea at once and concentrated our attention on Moss Ghyll side of the buttress, which was broken up by right-angled corners running upwards from west to east at a uniform angle of 65°. The nearest of these corners stopped us in less than 30 feet, but we were determined to try the next. It appeared difficult of access from this ledge; accordingly a descent to the Ghyll, and an awkward traverse from the top of the next pitch was effected. I climbed up this groove with some difficulty until the slab on the left almost gave out and upward progress seemed scarcely feasible; the groove immediately on my right continued upwards for a considerable distance, but the traverse into it appeared too difficult and I returned to Herford. We thereupon decided to give up the attempt and climb Pisgah Buttress instead. We did so with searching eyes on the rock face which had so successfully repulsed us, and I for one returned to Wasdale with the opinion that the Central Buttress would not go. . . .

[These became H. M. Kelly's superb Moss Ghyll Grooves—unclimbed until 1926.]

Consideration of other climbs which led up apparently impossible but actually feasible rocks, impressed on us the necessity of not judging by appearances, but of trying all places, however impossible or impracticable they looked. . . . We accordingly assured one another that, as we had not actually attempted the ascent of the 'Great Flake', there was still a chance of finding a feasible route up the Central Buttress.

It was not until June, 1913, that we had an opportunity of putting this theory into practice on the Central Buttress. It is, however, one thing to talk lightheartedly of trying to climb a narrow 40 foot crack, of which the top overhangs the bottom some 12 feet, and quite another thing to stand at its foot prepared to do so. The crack proper started some 30 feet above our grass ledge (the Oval) and obviously could be reached without great difficulty. I ascended about 25 feet and found myself below a large bulge in the side of the flake; I could have got over this bulge, but the sight of the crack above was too much for me, and Herford took my place and climbed to the foot of the crack. He also decided that to attempt to force it, without knowledge as to what lay above, would be unjustifiable.

I was abroad all that Summer, but Herford and Jeffcoat spent a profitable afternoon in exploration from above. From the top of Keswick Brothers' climb—below the variation finish—they traversed out on to the face of the Central Buttress, first downwards some 30 feet, and then horizontally to the right for about the same distance to a large flat rock, 'The Cannon', which is a conspicuous feature in the profile view of the face. From this point they descended a narrow shattered ridge for 40 feet to a good belay on an exposed platform known as Jeffcoat's Ledge, and a further descent of 12 feet gave access to a shelf of rock some 3 feet wide approximately, narrowing gradually down to 18 inches and supporting various large rock flakes in a state of doubtful equilibrium. Visually the ledge was concealed by a rather larger detached flake some 10 feet high and barely 3 inches wide at the top. Herford traversed out on the ledge climbed on to this detached mass, and walked along it and climbed down the opposite side. We now realised that he was on the top of the 'Great Flake' which formed the left retaining wall of the crack we had tried to climb from below. The flake narrowed down to a knife-edge, so thin and fretted that it was actually perforated in some places. Crawling carefully along it to the end Herford descended the overhanging crack, whilst Jeffcoat paid out rope from the belay. Unfortunately, the rope jammed during the descent and Herford had very great difficulty in getting down. He considered, however, that the crack was just climbable, and wrote me to that effect. Thus ended what is probably one of the most remarkable and bold explorations ever carried out in the district, and it is to be greatly regretted that Jeffcoat, who had lent such valuable assistance, was unable to join us in the actual ascent of the climb.

On April 19th of this year (1914) Herford, Gibson, Holland and myself returned to Scafell for the attempt. Herford and Gibson ascended Keswick Brothers' climb and traversed out on to the Central Buttress, whilst Holland and I climbed direct from Rake's Progress to 'the Oval'. Gibson lowered me a rope down the crack and after removing my boots I attempted the ascent. As far as the bulge, above-mentioned, the climbing was comparatively simple, but from this point to a large jammed stone 20 feet higher it was extremely difficult, as the crack is practically holdless and just too wide to permit a secure arm wedge. Two fairly good footholds permit of a position of comparative comfort just below the jammed stone and I noted, as Herford had suggested, that it was possible to thread a rope there. The stone itself afforded quite a good hand-hold, but the crack above overhung to such a shocking extent that the ascent of the remaining 12 feet proved excessively difficult. My arms gave out long before the top was reached and a very considerable pulling up from Gibson was required before I joined him. Herford then tried the ascent on a rope and just succeeded in getting up without assistance. We thereupon decided to attempt the ascent in orthodox manner, and preparatory thereto descended by Broad Stand and rejoined Holland on The Oval.

Our plan of attack was to climb up the crack and thread a loop behind the jammed stone, and I undertook to do this, if Herford would lead the upper part, which he was quite prepared to do. My first procedure was to soak two feet of the end of a rope in wet moss, to render it stiff and facilitate the threading. I then attempted the ascent, but six feet below the jammed stone found my position too precarious to be pleasant and called Herford for a shoulder. He came up without the least hesitation and, standing on the bulge at the foot of the crack, steadied my feet on small holds until I attained a safer position and was able to climb up to the chockstone. The stiff rope threaded very easily, and making a double loop I ran my own rope through it for the descent, which was, under those conditions, quite safe.

After a brief rest Herford tied on the threaded rope and speedily reached the level of the chockstone. He made a splendid effort to climb the upper part, but his strength gave out and he returned for a rest. A second equally fine effort was also unsuccessful, and he climbed down to The Oval. I then made one attempt, but soon abandoned it, and we unanimously agreed to postpone the ascent till the morrow, leaving a threaded rope in situ. As Holland had already spent seven hours on The Oval we decided to waste no more time; and accordingly descended via the traverse into Moss Ghyll.

The next day we climbed to The Oval direct from the Progress and one member ascended to the chockstone to renew the loop, which showed signs of wear from the previous day's use. We decided that combined tactics would be necessary, and accordingly ran a second rope through the loop. Herford tied on one rope and I on the other, whilst Gibson and Holland manipulated the respective ropes. I followed Herford closely up the crack and hung on to the loop whilst he used my shoulders as footholds. Directly he vacated them I climbed three feet higher and hung by my hands from the top of the chockstone, whilst he again employed me as footholds, which are most sorely needed at this point, for the crack is practically holdless and overhangs about 20 feet. A minute or two of severe struggling and he reached the top—to the great joy of all members of the party.

Herford thoughtfully hung a short loop over the top of the flake to assist us in the ascent, but even then we required much help from above, and it was with a sense of great relief that we found ourselves on the crest of the flake. Murray, who had been observing us from the recess with some interest, was delighted with an invitation to join the party, so we lowered him a rope down the crack and induced him to remove the threaded loop on the way up.

The crux of the great Central Buttress was so climbed. Having done enough that day, the team, joyful in victory, returned to Wasdale. There still remained some 150 feet of unclimbed and unexplored rock above, and conscientiously they returned on the

morrow to complete the climb. This they did successfully, returning to the climb above the Great Flake via Keswick Brothers'
climb.

Sansom finished his article thus:

> The Central Buttress climb as a whole, is extremely interesting and
> the situations absolutely unique. As regards difficulty: The direct
> ascent to the Oval from Rake's Progress is decidedly difficult and
> entails an 80 foot run out. The Flake Crack is unfortunately exces-
> sively severe and requires very careful management to render its
> ascent safe. The traverses and ascents on the upper wall are extra-
> ordinarily exposed, but not unduly severe, and the climbing is
> exceedingly enjoyable. The climb is certainly the longest in the
> district.

It was, of course, much more than interesting, being a breakthrough in climbing concept and difficulty. Although it had used
rope aid on the chockstone, to surmount the crux, it was undoubtedly the hardest route in Britain and remained Lakeland's
hardest route until the 1930s—in fact, it was first climbed without
using sling aid on the chockstone only in 1931, by Menlove
Edwards, and in this free form it warrants the grade HVS today.
To avoid the aid is difficult and precarious, for the final fifteen
feet of the Great Flake is to be either lay-backed (a technique
where the climber places his feet at the same level as his hands
holding the flake; he pushes against the wall with his feet, the
horizontal force keeping him in place; movement of the hands
facilitates, hopefully, upward movement) or jammed on insecure
hand jams. (Here the climber must expand his hand in the crack
by forming a fist, hopefully being able to lock his hand securely
enough to pull himself upwards.)

Climbing this route today, with all the modern equipment
available, is still very exciting. The moves above the chockstone
have to be made determinedly and boldly without hesitation.
When you look down to the scree some two hundred feet below
and realize that you are on plumb vertical rock, far too many feet
above your protection, it is almost impossible to believe that it was
climbed some seventy years ago. It is a fitting achievement to the
brilliance of Herford. There can be no doubt that the end result
of his techniques to climb the route, i.e. top-roping and pre-
inspection, more than justify the means.

C. F. Holland wrote his account of the climb much later, and it appeared in the 1921 Fell and Rock Climbing Club Journal. In it he tells of his first meeting with Herford:

Some few years ago, in 1913, to be exact, tired, dirty and dishevelled, I climbed wearily into one of the antique carriages that convey one from Bangor to Bethesda. Opposite me sat a tall young man of striking appearance, obviously alien in every way to the quarrymen and suchlike who filled the carriage, jabbering some strange language, presumably Welsh. According to the usual custom of the English under such conditions we did not exchange a single word, but when on reaching Bethesda we found we were both bound for Ogwen we agreed to share a vehicle, and the subsequent conversation that enlivened the somewhat slow progress to the cottage inaugurated a friendship that is now only a fragrant memory. My companion was S. W. Herford. The next day, my first with him in the mountains, showed me that I had met a man of highly unusual personality, initiative, and physical strength, while the masterly way in which he led the western Gully on Glyder Fawr demonstrated his superb qualities as a cragsman. Next day, his party arrived, and the good-natured refusal to allow me to stand out proved the thoughtful kindness and unselfishness that were so remarkable and engaging a part of his character.

He also brings to light in his article the fact that these early pioneers climbed all year round and in weather that many modern-day climbers would not venture forth in. In short, they were remarkably tough.

My acquaintance with this extraordinarily perpendicular cliff was made in January, 1914, when, one snowy afternoon, four of us, with Herford as leader, traversed out from the sheltered recesses of Moss Ghyll onto the great ledge that runs across the buttress some 80 to 100 feet above Lord's Rake.

Under the prevailing conditions, the expedition seemed to be a most perilous one, and the two corners we had to pass places of some severity, safe as they may be on a hot summer's day.

Eventually, we reached the belay near the end of the ledge, and prepared to rope down. As a matter of fact, Herford climbed down successfully, in spite of the snow, though he announced that it was pretty near the limit. When the third man had joined me at the belay, I told him I was going down strictly on the rope and, without waiting to ascertain whether he was ready for me or not, seized the rope with both hands, and more or less jumped over the edge.

As he was not ready, my descent was a remarkably rapid one, till I came to a stop some 25 feet lower with my feet on a ledge, or, as Archer Thomson would have put it, 'chanced on a knob of rock'. It will always be a proud memory that my ejaculation during this unexpected performance was 'God Save the King'. There are so many things one might have said and regretted. A little while previously I had surveyed in the gathering gloom the crack which was pointed out as a possible means by which the buttress might be ascended above the Oval, and summarily decided that it was impossible. Near Easter, however, I found to my horror that a serious attack on the buttress was contemplated, and that the attempt was to be made, not tentatively—there was little of the tentative in Herford's character—but with determination to succeed, if human beings could do so.

Holland continues graphically to describe the climb with his account of Herford surmounting the crux illustrating the perilous nature of the climb:

Sansom was hanging by indifferent sloping handholds on or near the lower end of the great chockstone, and Herford was standing on his shoulders, about to make the first step of the last tremendous solo effort. The initial difficulty confronting him was that of getting a purchase with his left foot in a groove unsuitably shaped for that purpose. Sansom's left hand began to slip under the great strain, and must inevitably have given way very soon, in which case he would have come off, though only for a foot or two, on to the loops. Herford's fall, unavoidable if this had happened, would have been a very serious affair indeed, and even if his rope had held it is impossible to see how we below could have given any assistance, beyond keeping the ropes tight, if either had been injured in any way.

   Finding himself unable to get his foot as he wanted it, Herford stepped back and accidentally put his foot on the slipping hand, thus holding it in position; and the difficult step was made so quickly at the second attempt that Sansom was able to support the double weight till that of the leader was removed.

Herford and Sansom were never to climb together again. After Central Buttress Herford accompanied G. Winthrop Young to the Alps. Despite poor weather they traversed the Matterhorn, ascending by the Mutt arete and descending by the ordinary eastern ridge (Hornli Ridge). They virtually soloed the entire mountain, roping up only for one two-hundred-foot section.

   At the outbreak of war Herford travelled to France to become a war correspondent. He could not, however, simply observe, and in November he served as chauffeur to the Red Cross Society. In February 1915 he enlisted in the 24th Royal Fusiliers (Sportsman's Battalion), was unbelievably refused a commission and on 28th January 1916 was blown to pieces by a rifle grenade, "He died as a private, he whom many would have gladly followed anywhere, to share the risk with whom was an honour and a privilege."

Of Sansom: he survived the bloody holocaust, first serving with the medical teams and then in 1915 joining the Royal Flying Corps, receiving both the MC and the DFC. He lived until March 1980, when he passed peacefully away at his home in Surrey, aged ninety-two.

After the war, though he returned to Wasdale, he missed Herford greatly and climbed mainly alone. He finished his article 'Goodbye to All That' thus: "As I am 87 this year, I fear that my climbing days are over, but my love for the Wasdale Fells will endure forever." The following poem, it is said, was written by G. S. Sansom:

> I will go back to the hills again
> That are sisters to the sea,
> The bare hills, the brown hills,
> That stand externally,
> And their strength shall be my strength
> And their joy, my joy shall be.
>
> I will go back to the hills again,
> To the hills I knew of old,
> To the fells that bare the straight larch woods,
> To keep their farms from cold:
> For I know that when the Spring time comes
> The whin will be breaking gold.
>
> There are no hills like the Wasdale hills,
> When Spring comes up the dale,
> Nor any woods like the Larch Woods,
> Where the primroses blow pale;
> And the shadows flicker quiet wise,
> On the stark ridge of black sail.
>
> I have been up and down the world,
> To Earth's either end,
> And left my heart in a field in France,
> Beside my truest friend;

And joy goes over, but love endures,
And the hills, unto the end.

I will go back to the hills again,
When the day's work is done,
And set my hands against the rocks,
Warm with an April sun,
And see the night creep down the fells,
And the stars climb one by one.

A greater contrast than the serenity and beauty of Wasdale and the bloody awful mess that was to become the Western Front is hard to imagine. The following article by C. T. Holland (Lieutenant) was written on leave from the trenches in 1916 and is entitled 'Pictures In the Fire':

As the car sped swiftly along the side of the lake it all seemed like a dream. Before me lay Wasdale with its picturesque little hotel in a nest of trees, the quaint cluster of fields looking more than ever like a jig-saw puzzle, and the surrounding hills asleep in the placid autumn sunshine. The Napes still clung to the side of Gable, Mossdale still preserved that melancholy which makes it a valley apart. With some brooding secret to be kept and mourned over, and the beck still murmured through the valley nothing seemed changed and the War was as if it had never been, the two long years since I was last here, with their vicissitudes, training, the journey to a strange land, the endless fatigues and dangers of active service, the terrible experiences, sorrow of seeing trusted friends suddenly struck down, were as a day that is quickly passed.

In the evening I sat alone and looked at the pictures in the fire, pictures of the 'dear dead days'. How it all came back to me! The happy circle sitting round the fire in this very room, the rapid ebb and flow conversation, talk of past performances, discussion of plans for the future, anecdote and friendly chaff, followed by foolish though absorbing games played with a rope slung over a beam, and attempts at hand balances and other follies fraught with danger to furniture, if not life and limb, until finally someone looks at the time which reminds us that if we would carry out the next day's plans it would be as well for us to get some sleep. And then comes a fall of coal, the flames leap up merrily and a succession of climbing memories passes before me. The weather changes as the pictures pass in a most amazing manner. At one moment all is delightful, the sun shines, the rocks are dry and warm and nothing seems too difficult. At another, an icy wind howls over the crags and snow fills every crevice and covers every hold, and now again the rain lashes down and down unmercifully and appears to be bent on washing us away and down to the bottom. Then in a breath the wind dies down, the rain stops, and the hills are shrouded in a dense mist that hides the crags as if to protect them from the impertinences of those who would peg into their recesses.

And now comes a train of more particular memories of Walker's Gully, encased in ice and very forbidding. I remember how we prepared to spend the night out in its gloomy cavern, our precautions consisting in taking a pair of socks and an extra sandwich apiece. However, the giant is conquered and that night the fireside seems all the more delightful for the memory of a truly Homeric struggle, during which Herford comes off, a little contretemps which merely amuses, as being an experience, for him, out of the common. The Pillar vanishes in the mist and now the rocks are covered with snow. We are in Moss Ghyll, and one by one make a separately difficult traverse onto the Central Buttress, along whose ledges we crawl with the utmost caution till a strong belay is reached when we rope down onto the Progress in rapidly gathering darkness. I am, I recollect, supremely thankful to be off that appalling ledge.

Again, I am on the ledge, but this time the weather is warm and bright, and I remain on it for seven hours, sometimes alone, sometimes with companions, and, that awful crack hanging over my head, as bad and awful as anything ever seen in a nightmare. And now the dreaded thing has actually happened and I am trying to climb it, but am soon reduced to confining my efforts to the three ropes that connect me with those above—I refer to my fellow-climbers not celestial beings.

And now comes a swiftly moving throng of memories, treading on one another's toes and jostling each other out of the light. The vast slabs on the Pinnacle gleam out in sunlight, but change instantaneously to a vicious crack on Pisgah Buttress and to dull hopeless stare of snow-covered rocks on a cloudy day. The gloom deepens and the Engineer's Chimney gives me a sensation as of one to be swallowed by a vast shark. Away fly the clouds and the Napes ridges rise up in swift succession, my toes tingling as I feel them wriggling about in the cracks below the Eagle's Nest, and again I wish I had never been born while clinging to minute irregularities outside the Abbey. A wicked slab below the Needle defeats me with monotonous regularity, while I grind my teeth and the flesh off my bones simultaneously, and the Arrowhead reminds me of Mr. Chevy Syme, the next step appearing to be always round the corner. All this time there have always been two things above me, a rope, and Herford at the end of it, as they are when finally I find myself on a most pernicious and unregenerate buttress not far from Kern Knotts, when after a series of most futile efforts I become entirely helpless and return to terra firma in a series of bounces strictly regulated by the tension of a rope and the movements of a pair of arms wielding it. The ultimate bump breaks the spell and all I see now is a face, the face of one who will never again be seen on the rocks he loved so well.

His memory will always live as long as rock climbing endures, not only as a great climber, but also as a great-hearted gentleman who gave his life for his country. By many of us he will be remembered as the finest and bravest man we ever knew.

May the memory of what he was be a stimulus and an incentive to those who are left to play the game both on the rocks and off them.

In two short years, 1912 to 1914, Herford had made an indelible mark not only on the history of climbing but also on his fellow climbers. J. Laycock wrote:

Before his time it was impossible in the Lake District to escape from the overpowering tradition of an earlier great climber, a previous standard, an earlier cult which defied comparison. Herford has eclipsed that standard and a new tradition has arisen. But all Herford's friends will be, as he himself would have been, the first to welcome the arrival of a greater climber still. However great he cannot love the mountains more than Herford did. And that is the thing that matters.

And Holland finished his article on the Central Buttress with the following remarks: "Alive he had no equal, dead his supremacy is still unchallenged. . . . I at any rate, firmly believe that the spirit of Herford is still abroad amongst the hills, and I know that some day I shall meet him there."

If one spring day on Scafell you should see fit and energetic young men, sporting Norfolk jackets, nailed boots and a hemp line, walking through the morning mists or hear their cheerful banter echoing round the sheer rock walls, do not be surprised if they make directly for the Great Central Buttress; it will only be Herford and Sansom re-united at last.

An interesting postscript recently occurred when in a disused chapel in Manchester, which was due to be knocked down, was discovered a stained-glass window dedicated to Herford. Fortunately it was rescued by the Fell and Rock Climbing Club and is now situated in the Eskdale Outward Bound School. It is an ideal location, where once again Herford can act as an inspiration to the many youngsters who will learn to love the fells.

Route name	Grade	Location	Comments
1912 Kern Knotts West			
Buttress	VS	Great Gable	G. S. Sansom led
Direct from Lord's Rake to Hopkinson's			
Cairn	S	Scafell	
Girdle Traverse	S	Scafell	Alt. with G. S. Sansom
1913 Wayfarer's Crack	S	Great End	
1914 Central Buttress	HVS	Scafell	Alt. with G. S. Sansom

6

Harry Moss Kelly
(20th May 1884–March 1980)

By the end of the First World War a considerable percentage of the British male population lay dead. Many active climbers who had shaped development prior to the outburst of hostilities were never to see their beloved fells again.

> Die, and feel their embers quicken
> Year by Year, in summer time;
> When the cotton grasses thicken,
> On the hills they used to climb.

Logically, one could assume that it would have been many years before the initiative was again taken. The converse was, however, the case. At the start of the 1920s the vacuum had been filled, and an unprecedented wave of development began.

It was as though there was not enough time to make up for those deprived and dark days in the trenches. Men and women revelled in the freedom of the hills. Gone were the inhibitions of pre-war days when only a mere handful of people could, or believed they could, climb the hardest routes. There began a period when many people consistently climbed hard.

Attitudes and techniques changed, and consequently standards increased. At the crest of this wave and markedly responsible for the new approach was Harry Moss Kelly. In retrospect it is clear that it was, significantly, he who was the originator of modern rock climbing.

Modern rock climbing is cool and calculating; it demands a rational approach rather than the death-or-glory style which, superficially, O. G. Jones displayed. Kelly was an unwaveringly enthusiastic climber who displayed a smooth and attractive style. Free from misconceptions and the influence of the preceding generation, he adopted an open mind and tackled the climbing game afresh.

Introducing new techniques, he created a controversy and at the same time revolutionized the climbing scene when he popularized the use of 'rubbers' for Lakeland climbing. Rubbers were plimsoles (pumps) with a soft rubber sole. The rubber gives tremendous grip in the dry and enables the climber to use friction holds that could not be used with the boots of his day. He had tried them out on his native gritstone and found them superior to 'nails'.

On 25th August 1915 he gave them a scientific comparison on his favourite gritstone outcrop—Castle Naize. He concluded: "It is much more difficult climbing in nailed boots than rubbers especially where holds are small and also necessitate high reach up of the foot." Having reached this conclusion, he wholeheartedly applied his philosophy, with devastating results.

The use of rubbers sparked off a tremendous debate on the ethics of doing so. Many people considered it to be cheating and would not accept that rubbers were far superior to nailed boots. Amazingly, people were still heatedly discussing this issue when I first started climbing in the late 1960s—almost fifty years after their inception!

Sid Cross, a great friend of Kelly, related to me a very amusing incident. It involved Kelly, late in life, and another pioneer of a previous era, one of the Woodhouse brothers, who was extremely deaf. Sid introduced them, and they seemed to be getting on famously, with the voice of Woodhouse considerably raised because of his deafness. Suddenly Woodhouse shouted out:

"Rubbers." It echoed round the room. "Never liked them," he continued. "Not playing the game you know!" He had quite forgotten that Kelly had been responsible for their introduction. Sid never heard what Kelly said, but the conversation continued on amicable terms for some time!

Attitude of mind is probably the most significant factor in rock climbing. You must gauge yourself and the problems clearly and without prejudice. Kelly had climbed throughout the war and had taken no part in the butchery. He was a Socialist and an agnostic. On the latter he kept an open mind and was by no means an atheist.

His wife, Emily, believed that women should be recognized as climbers in their own right and not just as the weaker party in a mixed climbing team. She founded the Pinnacle Club solely for women in 1921. Harry had no reservations, for he believed her to be correct, and he actively supported and encouraged her. In the early 1920s to accept the equality of women was a radical thing to do.

Kelly adopted a more sophisticated system of rope management and believed in safe climbing with sound belays—he was not averse to popping in the odd piton. His idea was to produce a good route on sound, clean rock, and if this required work to achieve, he would give it his all. Doggedly determined, he would go at a proposed line until he could climb it in good style from bottom to top (often he would reverse the route also). People today are under the impression that this is a recent development. It is not. Kelly, inspected, 'gardened', climbed in stages, etc, until he created a good route. ('Gardening' is the removal of loose rock, soil and grass from a proposed new climb. It is accomplished by descending from above, usually from the top of the crag, by rope. A climber may be lowered by his companions or more safely by abseiling down a rope fixed from above.) Two products of this attitude are Tophet Wall (S) on Great Gable and Moss Ghyll Grooves (HS) on Scafell. In my opinion, with the possible exceptions of Main Wall on Cyrn Las (Wales) and Integrity on Sron na Cich (Skye), these are the best routes of the grade anywhere in Britain.

Another of Kelly's great innovations was the concept of the practical guidebook. His series of Fell and Rock Climbing Club guides, started in 1923 with Pillar Rock, were the model that all subsequent definitive works have copied. He broke with tradition and replaced flowery, emotive and lengthy descriptions with those that were short, factual and straight to the point. The best way to illustrate this point is to examine a route description of the same climb before and after Kelly's editing.

From George S. Bower's 1922 *Dow Crags and Climbs around Coniston* FRCC guidebook we have:

Intermediate Gully—severe; strenuous; 80 feet rope.

There are members of the club to whom 'Intermediate' is more than a climb; rather is its ascent one of solemn rites connected with the practice of a cult. To one such disciple did I write, asking for a description of the preparations necessary on the part of those who would attain to this *cercle*. The reply came by wire: "Train on raw meat and stout, use Bulldog buttons. . . ." In the framing of the following notes, it has been assumed that the would-be climber is suitably prepared.

From Kelly's edited 1938 Dow Crag FRCC guidebook (written by A. T. Hargreaves and S. H. Cross):

INTERMEDIATE GULLY—270 feet. Severe. Strenuous. Leader needs 60 feet of rope. One of the finest gully climbs in the district.

Combined with the use of diagrams and a much improved format, this enabled climbers who had not previously known the area to go and quickly locate a route. Further than that, it inspired climbers to go and do routes knowing that the description and grade would be accurate. Climbs were now divided into six categories of difficulty: Easy, Moderate, Difficult, Very Difficult, Severe and Very Severe. Sitting at home, the would-be climber could now confidently plan his weekends, and this alone was a tremendous fillip to climbing development.

Predictably, Kelly was heavily censured, his critics claiming that climbing would be devalued because the, albeit succinct, descriptions were taking the adventure and romance out of climbing. On the contrary, they opened up the hills to a great many more people, ensuring, as Kelly always did, that they could have the fullest of days' climbing.

Kelly's very first routes were done in Wales during the August Bank Holiday 1913. They showed a pattern which he subsequently adopted for all his gritstone and Lakeland climbing days. He ascended V and Notch Arete and descended NorNor Gully.

He was thirty years old, and he had done his first climb up and his first climb down.

He first visited Wasdale Head at Christmas 1914 and inspected the Napes Needle but confined his activities to walking. From this period on he became tremendously active on the gritstone outcrops. These were readily accessible from his native Manchester, and he climbed every weekend, whatever. His first new Lakeland route came in September 1916. It was only a minor sortie: he soloed Gladstone Knott Chimney No. 2 at the head of the Langdale Valley.

Keeping a meticulous and beautifully presented diary (he even indexed it), he recorded many active days on gritstone and a number of new ascents. Testing both nails and rubbers, he developed a superb balance technique. The Lakes bug had, however, bitten hard, and he began spending his holidays in Wasdale and Langdale.

The main feature of his early Lakeland climbing was the great number of routes he accomplished in a day. On a typical day's climbing on Pillar Rock he did North West Climb in ascent, descended Slab and Notch, then went up North Climb and down Central Jordan. Never walking to the bottom of a crag, as most climbers do, he always descended a rock climb. Subsequently he wrote: "What a wonderful fillip the art of descending has given to rock climbing. Even the old climbs have become new because of this. . . ." He was most certainly influenced by Herford's 'Doctrine of Descent', and his list of first descents equalled that of his first ascents (some forty-eight new routes in the Lake District alone).

The 1916 Lakeland Christmas was a white one. The hills were covered deep with fresh, soft snow. Here at any rate there was peace and tranquillity. Kelly was staying at one of his favourite haunts, Stoole End Farm at the head of Great Langdale. On Friday 23rd December he and his two companions set off to ascend that classic winter climb Central Gully on Great End (Scafell). Kelly wrote the following account:

Friday 23 December Central Gully, Great End—Avalanche
    The snow was deep on the fells. Crag climbing was out of question and it was suggested the Great End Gullies for snow work. We accordingly made our way up Rossett Ghyll over Esk Hause and skirted the foot of crags until we reached the Central Gully. The

journey was laborious; it took us 3 hours to reach the mouth of the gully and rarely did we fail to sink up to our knees as we plodded on. We had lunch before roping up and it was very soon evident that trouble would arise owing to the poor condition of the snow. For in our efforts to reach the first work pitch we were up to our middles in it and once nearly smothered in a minor avalanche which rushed towards us and surged round in a most fascinating manner: we, however, warded danger off by scooping a trough in the snow to enable it to run easily past. We had not ascended many more feet when the final avalanche came. The only warning we got was our leader's cry of 'look out!' and immediately we were swept downwards off our feet, absolutely snowed under. Fortunately, the snow was steep upon the screes and there were no crags to fall over, consequently with the exception of a smothered feeling—goodness knows how many feet of snow were on top of us—the sensation was not unpleasant. I thought of the man mentioned by Whymper in 'Scrambles amongst the Alps' who was snowed under in a similar manner and breathed his way out and wondered whether we would have to do the same or should we be buried under feet of snow. It did not take very long to settle those questions for in what must have been about 10 seconds (it was afterwards computed that we must have been carried along for at least 200′) we found our way down a scree slope with our hands just above the snow—breathlessly enquiring the extent of each other's injuries. The sum total of which was a slightly twisted knee for one individual, a bruised thigh for another—the remaining member of the party escaping scot-free, excepting for the cramped feeling we all experienced. Which, no doubt was due to pressure of snow on our bodies. Number three had parted with his ice axe and after it had been retrieved we painfully commenced our journey back. Ere we reached Esk Hause a probable cause of the avalanche made itself felt in the form of a blizzard, which raged with tremendous force. Our outward deep footsteps were mostly obliterated and on account of the flying snow, which completely enveloped us, we had great difficulty in finding the guide post. Rossett Ghyll was reached slowly but surely and the descent proved very trying; at times we were simply floundering waist deep in snow and it was a great relief to reach Mickleden being much exhausted by our struggles with the elements. Despite our condition, however, we only exceeded our outward journey by half an hour and after a change of clothes and a good meal we could well afford to have our laugh and say to one another that we were glad to have had such an experience.

Kelly and his friends were fortunate to survive the incident relatively unhurt, although his twisted knee prevented him from climbing for some weeks afterwards. Some have been less fortunate, for deaths have resulted from similar incidents in this avalanche-prone gully. A year later Kelly was again out in winter conditions and climbed Kinder Downfall in the Peak District, cutting steps with a single long ice-axe.

During the summer of 1917 Kelly visited the Lakes on a number of occasions, and he was finding the hardest climbs easy. This was a result of his natural ability combined with intense gritstone 'training'. Of Sergeant's Crag Gully he said: "Classed as severe but with exception of one 10 foot pitch only a moderate difficult."

'Off' days from climbing (days when the crags were out of condition or a rest day) were spent bouldering. On the Boulder in Wasdale Kelly recorded fourteen climbs including a feet-first ascent. This boulder, situated close to the famous Wasdale Head, had been climbed upon from the very beginning, but Kelly took this bouldering to its logical conclusion. He was making very technical (hard) moves and finding problems on every spare foot of rock, showing that even bouldering, today considered a sport in itself, is no recent innovation.

Predominantly, however, he was climbing on grit. When he was not on the mountain crags, he frequented Castle Naize, Laddow, Stanage and many other gritstone outcrops. He also climbed on sandstone at Frodsham, Helsby and Alderley Edge. Castle Naize, was I think, his favourite, and this is where he compared the merits of nails and rubbers. The delectable scoop was ideal for such a trial. On Stanage High Neb he put up Overhanging Chimney and Inaccessible Crack and solved the problems of High Neb Buttress and the girdle. (He soloed the latter in fifteen minutes wearing plimsolls.) At Laddow his Tower Face and North Wall have become gritstone classics.

His companions on the Peak District gritstone included Stanley Jeffcoat, Rooke Corbett, William Walker and J. H. Doughty. Jeffcoat is probably best remembered for his Roache's Chimney and the ledge named after him on Central Buttress. Corbett was one of the Munroists (that is, a person who has ascended all of Scotland's peaks above 3,000 feet), and whose name had been similarly linked to the Scottish peaks above 2,500 feet. Walker was later knighted and became Lord Mayor of

Manchester. Doughty was one of Kelly's greatest friends, a mathematician and talented mountain writer. He and Kelly penned 'A Short History of Lakeland Climbing', which was published initially in the Fell and Rock Journal and then in a book entitled *The Hill—writings of J. H. Doughty*. Many subsequent articles have drawn their substance from this work.

Kelly was no mean writer himself, and he had ability to put both feeling and technical accuracy into his work. On Christmas Eve 1917 on Pavey Ark he made notes of his day's climbing and included in them the following remarks concerning Stickle Tarn:

Rocks streaming with water—slight thaw overnight. The tarn presented a wonderful sight. Had been frozen but ice was now being broken up by a strong wind blowing across the lake. One half of the latter was turbulent water whilst the other half was covered with ice. At junction were a number of ice floes one was reminded with aid of a little imagination very much of South Polar Scones (as described). One bank of tarn was heaped up with broken ice, evidently due to pressure of wind and water. This broken ice presented a unique spectacle, being apparently striped, which on inspection was found to be due to corrugation of one side; the depth of the corrugation being quite ½'' deep and 1½'' broad.

On the Boxing Day he made his way back to Manchester, and the following comments show his growing love for the fells with their unique qualities of balance and colour: "The colouring of the hills was beautiful. At times the reds were simply startling. Outlines of hills sank into heliotrope mist. Innumerable greens mixed up with browns and patches of snow here and there."

In 1918 Kelly was climbing actively and hard, but significantly he was beginning to notice unclimbed lines. He began to explore areas of rock and weigh up the potential of the Lakeland crags. After climbing all the Pinnacle Face routes (Scafell) in a day, he suggested that the many variations should be strung together and that really there were only two routes worth doing. Kelly was developing an eye for 'a line'. This quality is a complex function of knowing what rock remains unclimbed, what lines are possible and also worth climbing. To put theory into practice demands ability, determination and courage. Kelly was to show he had an abundance of these properties.

Of his day on the Pinnacle Face, 18th May 1918, he wrote: "The weather was sunny throughout and simply perfect for the

Pinnacle Face. Perhaps this made the famous climbs seem easy, maybe such climbing afforded by Tower Face (Laddow) had something to do with it."

Then one day in August that year he climbed a number of routes, finishing his climbing day by descending Botterill's Slab. His account continues as follows: "Mickledore 4.45 p.m. Scafell Pike 5.00 p.m. Esk Hause 5.30 p.m. Esk Pike 5.45 p.m., Bowfell 6.08 p.m. Three Tarns 6.17 p.m. Stool End via Band 6.42 p.m. Not a bad day altogether."

Kelly had served his apprenticeship, and the following year was to see a great new wave of development.

In 1919, then, began the great post-war renaissance—whose main participants included Bower, Roper and Kelly. Roper with Bower produced Great Central Route on Dow Crag, which was generally thought to be one of the hardest routes then climbed. A strenuous and awkward crack is followed by an impressively technical wall.

Kelly was, however, the most prolific and produced some ten new routes, five of which were at the highest standard—Very Severe. His companions included C. F. Holland, C. G. Crawford and R. E. W. Pritchard. Holland was a link with pre-war climbing, for he had been with Herford and Sansom on the great Central Buttress on Scafell. He and Crawford proved to be ideal companions for Kelly. Holland had the experience and Crawford was the cheerful optimist essential in any successful team.

They climbed every route then recorded on the Pinnacle Face (Scafell) and made a number of important variations. Kelly then focused his attention on Pillar Rock. There existed at the time only three routes on the magnificent west face, and their ascents had been spread over half a century. Within a fortnight Kelly both doubled this number and increased the difficulty a full grade.

Rib and Slab Climb (S) was led by Holland. Route 1 (Sodom) and Route 2 (Gomorrah) were very severe, led by Kelly, and amongst the hardest routes in Britain. The latter two routes were accomplished in a single day, and Kelly wrote an amusing yet gripping account entitled 'A Tale of a Pair of Rubbers'.

With Holland he led Route 1 without incident, but unfortunately Holland's well used and flimsy plimsolls fell to pieces during the ascent. The front half of the sole of each had detached itself from the uppers. As he walked along, the soles slapped the uppers, making a distinctive sound. The question was, should they attempt the first ascent of Route 2? The line they spied was formidable—following a series of natural grooves up the sheer and impressive west face. It was obviously going to be a hard climb. As on many great ascents, enthusiasm bettered discretion, and they went to it with a vengeance. For some unknown reason Holland thought it better not to wear the boots in which he walked up to the Rock. Of Holland's enforced climbing technique Kelly wrote: "Stepping onto a foothold he would jerk his knee upwards causing the dangling flap to do likewise then quickly slap his foot on the hold. All went well at first until the Sentry Box—i.e. flip-flapping up."

The pitch from the Sentry Box (a recess formed in the rock face where one can stand with something like security) was obviously going to be very hard. Kelly climbed a chimney then a vertical crack for fifty feet, until eventually he was forced right-wards onto an exposed rib of rock in the centre of the great wall. Locating a poor belay, he perched himself on the rib, with only an apology for a stance, and made himself ready to bring up Holland.

Kelly knew that the situation was serious. The pitch had been very hard, and he could not envisage Holland climbing the steep crack and delicate work beyond wearing broken plimsolls. Realizing that there was no alternative, Kelly remained unruffled and mentally prepared himself for Holland seconding the pitch.

Holland proceeded up the chimney as far as he was able. Then the 'flip-flap' holds ran out, and he was off. Kelly performed brilliantly and held Holland dangling at the end of the rope. Bracing his legs on inadequate footholds, he managed to swing Holland round until he was able to reach better holds. Pulling and manipulating, he brought Holland up to the stance and relative safety.

During the mêlée the rope knocked the pipe from Holland's mouth, and a dislodged stone hit him on the head. Kelly continued his account:

> Who would not explode under such circumstances? What with falling off; loss of pipe, and giving him what he described as a 'bloody coxcomb' I was well and truly put on the mat.
>
> Moreover, not only did I go about splitting open climbers' skulls, but, more heinous still, I had just committed, what was to him, the

unpardonable sin of using a split infinitive in my apologies for my remissness.

Holland had in the heat of the moment ignored the fact that both climbers were within a hair's breadth of disaster. They were still by no means safe, and it must have been an extremely determined and brave effort on Kelly's part to carry on and to lead them both safely to the top.

They coiled the rope and departed in silence, following the high-level route to Wasdale, passing Robinson's Cairn without "giving their habitual glance of homage before losing sight of the cliff for the day". As they speeded back, Kelly thought of the two first-class routes and the day that had been rather spoilt by his castigation. In the light of what finally transpired, he imagined Holland to be brooding over the omission to pay the customary tribute to the rock. Perhaps Holland was relating the incident to that story in the Bible where to look back was fatal, for as they both neared their base, Burnthwaite Farm, he shattered the silence by exclaiming: "Kelly, if you don't have names for those climbs, we've done today, I've got a couple." Kelly finished his article thus: "Relieved at this relaxation of the tension between us I gladly responded by asking what they were and got the significant reply—'Sodom and Gomorrah!' " These names were considered too controversial by the Fell and Rock Climbing Club, until they finally published them in the 1968 guide (forty-nine years after the event).

When the 1920s arrived, climbing really had entered a new phase. The routes once held in awe, climbed only by the likes of Jones, Botterill and Herford, now became ordinary. The general standard of climbing increased significantly.

That year Kelly produced another five routes. Typical of the new outlook was his determination to climb that beautiful buttress of rock on Great Gable known as Tophet Wall. The saga began on 30th August 1920 and continued until 14th July 1923. Finally the result was a climb that is simply magnificent. Not particularly hard, now graded Severe, it looks impressive and gives superb movement with situations to match.

Extracts taken from Kelly's diaries show the modern approach to the problem:

Monday 30th August, 1920
Exploration of Tophet Wall

Made an attempt on this. Started up a steep wall for about 12 feet got within 8 feet of top of a flake like rock (good stance belay at top as found afterwards). Crack looked too exposed so retired. Went up hellgate about 100′ then traversed to left along juniper and bilberry, came to a number of loose blocks (Pritchard joined me here) threw those down, did considerable amount of gardening. Self descended wall for about 60 feet in a diagonal direction and found myself above 'flake like rock' previously mentioned. Climbed back to Pritchard testing good piton (a ⅓ of the way en-route) and found it quite safe. Useful as a belay if pitch is led. Did not explore any further than this.

Friday 13th September, 1920
Further Exploration of Tophet Wall

Explored wall from above descended Ridge (Tophet) some 150′ to 200′. This Ridge lies immediately on sky line to left of Great Hell Gate Pinnacle. We had previously ascended it for about 100 feet to a point below a bulge. On this occasion I got down to the bulge about 15′ above the point, reached from below. On returning to Holland I investigated the upper part of what should be (if it goes) the Tophet Wall climb and also a route up a slab or wall en-route. We afterwards went to the foot of the Ridge and I endeavoured to overcome the bulge by standing on McFarland's shoulders but without success. Much disappointed as we anticipated this would go now we knew that all was plain sailing above.

Tues 7th September—Exploration of Tophet Wall
Sunday 12th September—More Exploration of Tophet Wall
May 1921 Prospected Tophet Wall
July 14th 1923 Tophet Wall (a) first ascent. H. M. Kelly and R. E. W. Pritchard.

I forgot to mention that Pritchard just got up from Hell Gate to see me finish off the climb and had thoughtfully carried a basket of strawberries up. A new climb followed by strawberries at the foot of it—what more could one wish for!

And the sweet fulfilment of his ambition.

During this period of intense climbing activity Harry Kelly suffered a great personal tragedy, for in 1922 his wife, Emily, was killed. It was a most unfortunate accident, and like many such accidents seemingly inexplicable, for she slipped whilst descending along the easy Tryfan's Heather Terrace.

She started climbing in 1914 and eventually climbed Lakeland's hardest routes. An exceptionally bold balance climber, she

was on the first ascent of Tophet Bastion S (Great Gable) and
made a number of distinguished solo ascents. Their friend J. H.
Doughty wrote:

> But it was perhaps on her beloved Derbyshire gritstone that she was
> most at home. Here you might see her any weekend, a slim, frail
> looking figure, in sober brown and grey that blended with the hue of
> the rock, gracefully poised on minute holds, or moving with easy
> effortless progress over some smooth slab, and seeming withal not an
> alien intruder, but rather some native genus of the crag itself.

H. M. Kelly wrote:

> My wife commenced her climbing career at the beginning of 1914, so
> that she had for some time found her feet when the Pinnacle Club
> was formed. Most of our gritstone climbing was done solo, hers
> particularly, from choice, as she wished, to use her own words 'to
> develop her own technique in her own way'. Perhaps her most
> outstanding climb was done on a Sunday in 1921 when she climbed,
> solo, Jones' Route from Deep Ghyll to Low Man as well as Profes-
> sor's Chimney. I wasn't there at the time but Holland, who was sitting
> on the top of Scafell Pinnacle with others, describes in an article he
> wrote afterwards to the Fell and Rock Journal, their consternation of
> seeing this lonely figure coming up the arete!

During this period Harry Kelly started staying at Eggerslack
Cottage near Grange-over-Sands, a wooded and retiring area,
well served by train, on the fringe of the Lake District. He also
took the first of his many climbing trips abroad. Norway, in
particular, with its deep fjords and snow-topped granite peaks,
seemed to capture his imagination; he returned many times. The
Alps too received his attention, and in 1928 he climbed with Eric
Shipton in Switzerland.

During the summer of 1930 he attempted to visit Russia and
climb in the Pamirs. He spent a frustrating week battling with
officialdom at the border but finally lost patience and returned to
England. For a committed Socialist it must have been a rather
sobering experience.

Although his British climbing was concentrated in the Lakes,
he frequently visited Wales and Scotland and never forsook his
native gritstone. He had a great affinity with the mountains, and
the following account of an early visit to Skye, recorded in his
diary on 9th September 1924, reveals this well:

Left M/c 11 p.m. met R. E. W. Pritchard at Wigan. Rather cold journey to Kyle of Lochalsh sprinkling of snow on the hills very fine colouring. Heather a glorious purple. Bracken touched with its first gold. Rowan trees scarlet with abundance of berries. Blue grey rock of most of the mountains and the lighter reddish sandstone of the Ben Eighe groups. What a glorious journey is the line from Dingwall to Kyle of Lochalsh, and what more glorious than the first view of the Cuillin down Carron with the afternoon's sun behind them. A great compensation for a tiresome journey. Took boat to Broadford (3/–) where we were met by Campbell's man who motored us over to the Sligachan Hotel.

Pritchard felt he was fortunate in having clear view of Sgurr Nan Gillean!

Fortunately, the Lakes became Kelly's greatest love, and he produced many more new routes, two of which were again exceptional. He wrote:

My first real climbing holiday in the Lakes was at Great Langdale at Easter 1916, although I had visited Wasdale at Christmas 1914. Until 1922 my holidays were roughly divided between Wales and the Lake District. I preferred the latter for longer spells and began to think that there was no place like Wasdale Head. I lost my heart to it so that when Morley Wood tried to inveigle me back to Wales by talking about 'a mighty unclimbed cliff' called Clogwyn du'r Arddu, I am afraid that I turned a deaf ear to his entreaties!

The exceptional routes were of course Moss Ghyll Grooves (HS) on Scafell and Grooved Wall (VS) on Pillar Rock. Moss Ghyll Grooves is generally reckoned to be Kelly's finest achievement. An elegant and bold climb, it follows for 265 feet an obvious system of grooves which slip slightly leftwards out of Moss Ghyll. The line separates the impressive Central Buttress wall from the lesser walls confining the great rift of Moss Ghyll.

It finally succumbed to Kelly on 1st July 1926, some seven years after his initial conception of its feasibility. Like Tophet Wall it had been a keen campaign with numerous inspections and attempts. The successful party consisted of Mrs Blanche Eden-Smith and J. B. Kilshaw ("a keen youth but with little or no experience", wrote Kelly).

Kelly wrote in his diary: "Explored Moss Ghyll Grooves from above, self climbed down to first groove and descended it about 15 to 20 feet gardening en-route. Saw enough to satisfy me that lower portion might be linked up with this—a matter of about 30 feet. Rejoined others."

Typically they descended down Keswick Brothers climb to reach the bottom of the crag and so approach Moss Ghyll Grooves. The lower section of the climb 'went' without any problem, but high on the middle of the slab the crux was reached. "From a very narrow foothold on the centre of the slab, a left-hand movement had to be made upward and outward to a small but level stance (the Pedestal) on the extreme edge, about two strides away."

Mrs B. Eden-Smith wrote:

> The difficulty lay in the fact that there was nothing to stride on except a small protuberance about the size of a damson stone, on which, moreover, hands had to be changed somehow. Twice Kelly tried it and came down to the grass for a rest from the toe-cramping foot-holds from which the movement must start. The third time he went straight for it and seemed just to flow over those two 'holdless' strides to the pedestal, where, at last, both feet could rest at once. The earnest pathos in his voice, as he besought his followers to do their best when their turn came, was ominously indicative of what he thought of the place.

Kelly wrote of the climb and of Mrs Eden-Smith's performance:

> This readiness to face any risk was also exemplified when she and I made the first ascent of Moss Ghyll Grooves. In order that the leader might avoid a run-out of about 80 feet (from the Oval to the Lookout) she undertook a precarious and belay-less stance some 15 feet higher, thereby boosting the morale of the leader. How much easier it was with someone at hand, to take that delicate step across the Pedestal!

The climb was in the bag. Above awaited a hundred-foot run-out of rope, but the ground was familiar, and the crux, Kelly knew, lay behind them. "Seven years of intermittent hope and thought crystallised, almost unexpectably, into achievement. Youth and maturity found equal delight, from their several points of view, in victory," wrote Kelly.

He thought the climb 'Very Severe' and slightly harder than Botterill's Slab. It undoubtedly is a great route but the passage of time and the subsequent cleaning of unfound rock and vegetation, plus the use of modern protection, have ensured that the climb is now marginally easier. It is remarkable that such an imposing and bold line is available to the many climbers with HS/HVS ability.

In 1928 Kelly was back on the Pillar Rock. Much work and gardening produced one of his best Very Severe routes. Grooved wall lies to the right of Walker's Gully and is well named. It is a fine climb, both technical and exposed, bearing all the hallmarks of a Kelly classic.

The following extracts taken from his diary show the tremendous amount of work and dedicated enthusiasm that may be required to produce a modern rock climb:

1928 Thursday 26th April
Exploration of Grooved Wall of Walker's Gully
H. G. Knight, W. G. Standring and Self
Made the belay, just below the wall on North East Climb at the end of the 6th pitch the base of operations. Extensive grubbing in the Long Groove about 120 feet down to the overhang at the bottom of the groove. The latter now looks presentable. We then descended the North East and then tried the proposed new route from the foot of the cliff. Reached the big flake once again. Knight led whence—self took lead to grass ledge below the overhang and was joined by Knight. Could make nothing of this despite desperate efforts by both of us. So rather tired party retracted at 6.30 p.m. after 5½ hours hard labour.

Saturday 28th April
Grooved Wall-Pillar
Self, H. G. Knight, W. G. Standring. Knight led last groove.
Before starting the climb we went up the W.G. again and Standring spent 2½ hours giving the long Groove and the ledges below a final sweep up. He continued down to the top of the Big Flake where he was to await us on our descent of the North East. When we arrived at the foot of the crag however he called that he was coming down from the flake for a drink which was not surprising after his early exertions.

He summarized the situation accordingly:

The party spent 8 hours in cleaning up the climb. There was enough earth sent down into Ennerdale to provide soil for the whole of the re-afforestation scheme. All climbers should be grateful for the work put in by Standring and Knight, for without the abnormal terrier-like qualities they displayed on this occasion the Grooved Wall as a climb would not exist.

There were of course failures, and during his early days he was repelled from O. G. Jones's famous route—Kern Knotts Crack (MVS). He soon made good and not only climbed but immediately reversed the route also. Strangely he never climbed Central Buttress (Scafell).

He attempted Central Buttress with Gibson in June 1919 when he was at the height of his climbing powers. They both reached the chockstone and retreated. "No enthusiasm in party for threading rope so gave attempt up. Traversed off Oval to Moss Ghyll." Then in 1921 on 20th August he was back again. He wrote:

> Bowen and I went up to Scafell to prospect Central Buttress. Found Frankland and Beetham already on the job. We went round by Keswick Brothers and down from Cannon onto flake. Learned there from Frankland and Beetham below they had already threaded two ropes behind chockstone on Great Flake. Beetham then climbed up on one rope and lashed himself to chockstone. Frankland then followed and climbed over Beetham to top of flake. We were asked to join on to their rope below Jeffcoat's Ledge and did so finishing rest of climb with them.

This was the now famous second ascent by that great climber C. D. Frankland (who was later killed when he fell from an easy climb on Great Gable) accompanied by the pioneer of Borrowdale climbing, Bentley Beetham. Kelly never bothered with the route again. He had ample opportunity but seemed no longer interested.

During the 1930s he continued to climb extensively. He formed a strong friendship with Sid and 'Jammy' (Alice) Cross, and they produced a number of new routes together. In 1938 Kelly climbed his last new route, the Rampart (HS) on the Scafell Shamrock; Sid Cross led.

Many may consider that Kelly had been granted a new lease of life. I think, however, that great climbers never lose their affinity for the mountains, for his last Lakeland climb was Holly Tree Traverse (VD) on Raven Crag, Langdale, on Thursday 4th July 1957. He was seventy-three years old.

He was a great balance climber, bold and inventive. There burned inside him an unextinguishable enthusiasm for mountains and climbing. Not only did he produce superb climbs but he also generated, with his revolutionary ideas, a wave of development that during the 1920s set the standard of Lakeland climbing above that of any other mountain area. His innovations of rubbers, gardening and cutting "the romantic nonsense" out of guidebooks lifted rock climbing out of one great era and into another. He undoubtedly was the originator of modern rock climbing.

When somebody operates on a different plane—that is, leads the field—extremes of character can be expected. Kelly was sometimes described as a tyrant and dictator among fellow climbers. He was certainly very single-minded, a man whom nobody would cross.

His meticulous edition of the Fell and Rock Climbing Club guidebooks brought criticism, but the result was a superb set of guidebooks, on which all subsequent modern guides are now modelled. A later Buttermere guide writer, Bill Peascod, said: "On receiving my draft back after Kelly's editing almost every word would be changed. At first this was disconcerting, but after reading his version there was no doubt it was better, clearer and more easily understood."

The other face of Kelly was warm and understanding: he was very fond of children and animals and they of him. When staying at the Old Dungeon Ghyll, he would spend a day entertaining the children there. In his diary he includes an account of sharing his sandwiches with a group of hill ponies. He lived for climbing, music and cricket and was a happy man, often singing, who created his own destiny.

There is a saying in England that a dog always reflects the character of its master. Harry Moss Kelly's beloved dog was a bull terrier, named Susie, who loved to be among the fells. There is no more ferocious, 'game' or determined breed of dog. Kelly died at the great age of ninety-six, in March 1980, specifying that there should be no charade, no celebrated funeral. His climbs remain and his memory also.

Route name	Grade	Location	Comments
1916 Gladstone Knott Chimney No. 2	D	Langdale	
1919 Low Man of the Right Wall of Steep Ghyll	MS	Scafell	C. F. Holland led
Waiting Room from First Pitch in			

Route name	Grade	Location	Comments
Steep Ghyll	MVS	Scafell	C. G. Crawford led
Tophet Bastion	S	The Napes	
Rib of Slab Climb	S	Pillar Rock	C. F. Holland led
West Wall Climb	VD	Pillar Rock	
Sodom (Route 1)	VS	Pillar Rock	
Gomorrah (Route 2)	VS	Pillar Rock	
Kern Knotts Buttress	VS	Kern Knotts	
Central Climb	S	Kern Knotts	
Flake Climb	VS	Kern Knotts	
1920 Upper Deep Ghyll Buttress	VS	Scafell	
Central Route, Deep Ghyll Slabs	S	Scafell	
Nook Wall Climb	S	Pillar Rock	
The Slab Climb	S	Lower Kern Knotts	
Sabre Ridge	VD	The Napes	
1921 Raven Route	MS	Dow	
1922 Red Ghyll Buttress	VD	Scafell	W. Eden Smith led
1923 Hind Cove Buttress	VD	Hind Cove—Pillar Area	
Slab Climbs Route 1 and 2	D	Hind Cove—Pillar Area	
The Appian Way	HS	Pillar Rock	
Forked Gully (right fork: ascent and descent)	HS	Buckbarrow—Wasdale	
Right Face Climb	HS	Buckbarrow—Wasdale	
Hidden Gully (Descent only!)	HS	Buckbarrow—Wasdale	
Tophet Wall	S	Great Gable	
1924 Wall and Crack Climb	VD	Pike's Crag, Scafell	
Juniper Buttress	VD	Pike's Crag, Scafell	
Southern Corner	S	Pike's Crag, Scafell	
The West Route	M	Lower Kern Knotts	
1925 Rib and Gully Climb	D	Hind Cove—Pillar Area	
Castor	M	Scafell Crag	
Pollux	VD	Scafell Crag	
The Bannister	E	Red Ghyll Buttress-Scafell	Blanche Eden-Smith led
Sinister Ridge	HVD	Black Crag—Scafell	
Hole and Corner Gully	M	Black Crag—Scafell	
Dexter Slab	HVD	Black Crag—Scafell	
Intermittent Chimney	M	Scafell—Shamrock	R. E. W. Pritchard led
Tower Buttress	S	Scafell—Shamrock	

Route name	Grade	Location	Comments
1926 Moss Ghyll Grooves	MVS	Scafell	H. M. Kelly, Blanche Eden-Smith and J. B. Kilshaw
1928 Long John	MVS	The Napes	H. G. Knight led, H. M. Kelly last man
Kern Knotts Chain (L. to R.)	VS	Kern Knotts	H. G. Knight led, H. M. Kelly last man
Kern Knotts Chain (R. to L.)	VS	Kern Knotts	H. G. Knight led, H. M. Kelly last man
Grooved Wall	VS	Pillar Rock	H. G. Knight led, last pitch W. G. Standring
1931 Plaque Route	D	Bowfell Buttress	
Central Route	HS	Bowfell Buttress	
1934 Pulpit Rock	VD	Pillar Rock	A. S. Piggot led
1937 Half Nelson Climb	S	Eagle Crag, Buttermere	Sid Cross led
Double Cross Route	VS	Eagle Crag, Buttermere	Sid Cross led
1938 The Rampart	HS	Scafell—Shamrock	Sid Cross led

7

A. T. Hargreaves
(1903–52)

The early 1930s were relatively unproductive years in the Lakes. The twenties men had had their day, and the death of Maurice Linnel on Ben Nevis in 1934 shook the climbing establishment.

Only four new courses were recorded in 1930, and three of these were attributed to a new name, A. T. Hargreaves. They were three excellent routes and, what was not realized at the time, one of them was exceptional.

The routes were Deer Bield Crack, reported as Severe and climbed on 16th February, Direct Route (Mild Very Severe) on Castle Rock–South Buttress, climbed on 30th May and Route 1 on White Ghyll, climbed on 15th September. Direct Route and Route 1 are very pleasant climbs, small classics in their way, and very popular today. Deer Bield Crack, however, was remarkable. Graded HVS today, it was probably one of the hardest climbs in the Lake District at that time, comparable with Central Buttress on Scafell and Black Wall on Dow Crag, the crux pitch being a wide chimney that had to be back-and-footed for forty feet. Very technical, it remains a serious and precarious piece of climbing even by modern standards. Climbers who go to the back of the chimney seeking protection usually fail. The way to do it is to grit your teeth, face right and go straight up the crack back-and-footing, not stopping until the belay is reached. Livesey recently described the climb as "Hargreaves' horror route of the 30's", expressing exactly many people's feelings when attempting the pitch. Even if this pitch is successfully negotiated, there remains a hard final pitch. Desperate and fingery to start, there is a long reach to a thin crack; the final wall overhangs in two directions. Joe Brown went to climb the crack in 1950. This is what he wrote in *The Hard Years*:

> We first went to Deer Bield Crag because its Crack was reputed to be one of the hardest climbs in the Lake District. The crag was also noted for drying off quickly after prolonged bad weather. The party was Slim, Wilf, Nat and Don Cowan. As we approached the crag, which could be seen from a long way off, a mystery developed. The crag was shining green, like an old Norman Tower pitted with lichen. The rocks were coated with green slime. No one liked the look of it at all.
> The crux of Deer Bield Crack was a smooth, narrow chimney. Being short and agile I brought my knees up to the chest and wriggled up in a wedge position. When the others arrived in the most difficult place in the chimney a tinkle of nails dropping out of their boots joined the sounds of their grunts and groans. Wilf came up first, fell off fifteen feet below me and elected to haul himself up on the rope. He sprawled on the stance in a black mood. . . . Don Cowan made furious scraping noises; his nails clattered down the chimney in a small shower. As soon as Don skipped off, the rope went tight and Wilf brightened up. 'Didn't I tell you, Don,' he yelled, 'the only way to get up this lot is to pull on the rope.'
> Nat Allen put up a tremendous struggle; sounds of a fierce battle drifted up . . . now everyone was shouting instructions to the weary warrior. If this was calculated to make Nat fall it succeeded. In spite of frivolity the entire party came up like sacks of potatoes. We were a dreadful sight, covered with grease from the crag.

The reason for such a dynamic ascent may be found in A.T.'s background. He had been thoroughly trained on, and was, a highly proficient gritstone climber. A Lancashire lad, A.T. was born in Rochdale in 1903. He first climbed in his twenties when he visited Laddow Rocks. By the beginning of the 1930s he had put up a number of notable gritstone routes. On Stanage Hargreaves's Black Slab Route and Christmas Crack stand out. On Laddow Rock Tower Arete was done and later Priscilla. One of the founder members of the Manchester University Climbing Club, formed in 1928, A.T. was grouped with Maurice Linnel and other keen gritstoners. He was also closely connected with the Rucksack Club.

A.T. took a job as a commercial traveller in Barrow and due to good fortune resided in the same street as George Bower, a fellow Rucksacker, and Bill Clegg, both important Lakeland climbers in their time. He had a company car and spent all his leisure time in the hills, repeating all the hardest routes of the day. He did an early ascent of Central Buttress with Maurice Linnel and Herbert Hartley.

In 1931 A.T. joined Linnel to descend Gimmer Crack and also made the second ascent of Joas-VS on Gimmer (the route's name being derived from the fact that it is of fairly lowly grade except for Just One Awkward Step).

A year later, climbing with G. G. Macphee, he produced the Nor'nor'west Climb (VS) on Pillar Rock, giving a particularly fine and exposed climb. September saw the same pair on Bowfell Buttress, and they did what was probably the best natural line up the front of the Buttress-Sinister Slabs. Again this was graded VS but it is now rated HS.

The year 1933 was a very important one in Lakeland climbing. It was really the year that the East Buttress of Scafell was opened up, and it heralded new attitudes and brought fresh realization of what was possible. The East Buttress is most certainly one of Lakeland's most impressive pieces of rock. It is steep and over-hanging, being the shape of a barrel laid on its side. Additionally the ground below sweeps down to Mickledore Beck in a series of rock steps and broken scree in such a manner as to leave any climber standing at the foot of the cliff in an already precarious position.

It really started with Colin Kirkus (the great Welsh pioneer) who in 1931 forced the most brilliant and serious Mickledore Grooves (VS) on the far right-hand side of the crag. Then, in 1932, Maurice Linnel with Sid Cross, then only seven-teen, climbed the Great Eastern Route (VS). But 1933 saw a con-solidation of these efforts, and Linnel went on to lead Overhanging Wall, seconded by A. T. Hargreaves. The route was aptly named and was the first really to attack the alarming barrel-shaped walls. Unfortunately Linnel used a piton on the second pitch. He explained his action in the Rucksack Club Journal of 1934:

> There was only one thing for it, and it was an eventuality for which I had come prepared. I inserted a piton in the little crack and inserted it well and truly, with a hammer. Nor was it only put there as a safeguard: by pulling on it sideways, downwards, outwards and upwards and finally planting a foot on it I was able, with a struggle, to reach a little ledge. I offer no apologies; those who prefer to climb the place unaided are cordially invited to remove the piton and do so.

(Although the piton remains in place, the climb is now done free by most parties.)

Then in August A. T. Hargreaves went back to lead an impressive series of ramps leading left across the face. The climb 'Morning Wall' (VS) was a very obvious natural line. He was accompanied by S. Clegg and, purely by chance, by Linnel, whom they had met at the foot of the crag. Linnel did not think the line would go, but of course A.T. proved him wrong. A.T. persisted on the East Buttress and with Linnel attempted the line that is now May Day Climb (HVS), Jim Birkett's first route, but they failed on the very technical initial slab.

These early days of A.T.'s reflect his rock-climbing ability but he was also a proficient mountaineer, being very able on snow and ice. At these activities he was active not only in Lakeland but in Scotland and the Alps. His Ben Nevis climbs are noted in Clark and Pyat's *Mountaineering in Britain*:

> The standard of difficulty of both rock and snow and ice climbing was consistently raised during the 1930's, three landmarks standing out distinctly from the steady progress of rock work. The first was the ascent of Route 1 on Cairn Dearg by A. T. Hargreaves and G. G. Macphee in 1931 and the ascent of Rubicon Wall, led by Hargreaves two years later. Either ascent, taken on its own, might have been merely the solitary exception; taken together they confirm that Lake District standards of rock climbing were at last being applied to Scotland.

A.T. first met a young Kendal lad by the name of Sid Cross on Dow Crag in 1931. A.T. introduced himself, and Sid with his very dry wit said: "Aye, I met your brother A. B. Hargreaves and

Alf Bridge on Gimmer—they followed us up Hiatus, I told them they were past it!" A.T.'s reply was instantaneous: "It is one thing to acknowledge A.B. as a friend, but certainly not as a brother!"

Sid and A.T. soon became the closest of friends, and he recalls that A.T. was always an immaculate climber, very straight and extremely tough. "He would not suffer fools, but if you were genuine then you couldn't ask for a better friend."

They both relished winter climbing, and A.T.'s ability to withstand cold and uncomfortable conditions was legend. Some very impressive Lakeland winter ascents fell to this team, and these included Steep Ghyll on Scafell, Central Gully on Great Gable, with the direct finish, numerous ascents of Moss Ghyll on Scafell and Pisgah Buttress on Scafell.

To put these routes into context, Steep Ghyll is today rated at winter grade IV/V, and to my knowledge Pisgah Buttress has never had a second winter ascent. Sid recalls: "A.T. was a real technician, cutting steps was done absolutely methodically and with a minimum of effort. I remember on Pisgah Buttress A.T. used a pan scrubber to remove verglas from the fingerholds." It must be remembered that for most of these routes they merely had a very long ice-axe and a pair of nailed boots. In later years, when Sid first went to the Alps, he made his own crampons especially for the occasion.

As for A.T.'s 'straightness', when camping on Ben Nevis one winter, Sid with his wife, Alice ('Jammy') Cross, climbed Tower Ridge. They took the Great Tower direct, climbing right over the top of it to gain the Tower Gap. The actual route lies round the east side of the Tower and is straightforward but spectacular. They eventually finished the route in the early hours of the morning. Returning to camp, they were met by A.T., who was just organizing a rescue party. A.T. asked what had kept them, and Sid explained the difficulties, adding that he thought he had only managed to get up with help from the Almighty. A.T. commented: "Why should that bugger look after you and nobody else?" (Maurice Linnel was killed on Ben Nevis in 1934 when he was avalanched at the top of Castle Climb.)

As for his toughness and ability to withstand cold, Sid reckons he only equalled A.T.'s performance one winter when Ruth Hargreaves was in hospital. A.T. visited her during the day, and this only left time for mountaineering in the late evening! One night they skied over Helvellyn and were descending down Swirral Edge in appalling conditions; they had not set off until midnight, and Sid was so cold that tears were streaming from his eyes. "I looked at A.T. and was very satisfied when I saw he was in a similar state of agony!"

A.T. and Sid Cross, along with their wives, Ruth and Jammy, opened the Burnmore Inn at Eskdale. They were co-authors of the Dow section of the Dow Crag, Great Langdale and outlying Crags guide published in 1938, and A.T. wrote the prestigious Scafell guide, published in 1936.

Another dozen new routes followed (on some they were accompanied by their wives), but few compared with their earlier achievements, although Prow of the Boat (HVS), led by Sid on 2nd June 1940, accompanied by A.T., Ruth and Jammy, was a good and technical line. Both Ruth Hargreaves and Jammy Cross were good climbers in their own right. Jammy was actually the first lady to lead Central Buttress (1939). A.T.'s last new routes were done in 1941, and again they were with Sid.

Known as 'the Innmates', they built up a large climbing clientele. Later the Crosses moved to the Old Dungeon Ghyll, and the Hargreaves stayed at the Burnmoor. During this period they became engrossed in ski-mountaineering. On the first day of a skiing holiday in Austria the Hargreaves and the Crosses were descending from the Hohe Mutt (above Overgurgh) when the snow slope avalanched. Tragically A. T. Hargreaves was killed. It was 1952 and A.T. was forty-nine years old.

	Route name	Grade	Location	Comments
1930	Deer Bield Crack	HVS	Deer Bield, Easdale	Reported climb as S
	Route 1	S	White Ghyll, Langdale	
	Direct Route	MVS	Castle Rock	
1932	Sinister Slabs	HS	Bowfell Buttress, Langdale	
	Nor'nor'west Climb	VS	Bowfell Buttress, Langdale	
1933	Overhanging Wall	VS	East Buttress, Scafell	M. Linnel led— one peg aid
	Morning Wall	MVS	East Buttress, Scafell	
	Hadrian's Wall	MVS	Pillar Rock	
	Ledge & Groove Climb	MS	Pillar Rock	

	Route name	Grade	Location	Comments
1936	Jacob's Ladder	HS	Scafell	
	Grey Bastion	MVS	Pike's Crag, Scafell	Sid Cross led
1937	Sector	MS	Pike's Crag, Scafell	Alt. leads
1938	Brimstone Buttress	MVS	Tophet Crag, Great Gable	
	Crocks Crawl	VD	Dow Crag	
1939	The Citadel	VS	Pike Crag	Family party
	Sirloin Climb	S	Pillar Rock	
	Wailing Wall	MVS	Pavey Ark, Langdale	Sid Cross led
1940	Shamrock Tower	MVS	Pillar Rock	Sid Cross led
	Prow of the Boat	HVS	Boat Howe Crag, Great Gable	Sid Cross led. Family party
1941	Red Ghyll Wall	MS	Scafell	
	Tower Postern	S	Scafell	Sid Cross led

8

Jim Birkett

(26th April 1914–   )

In the late 1930s and 1940s climbing standards rose dramatically yet protection techniques were virtually non-existent. In most cases the difference in leading a pitch and soloing was only the weight of the rope.

Climbing too was still very much a gentleman's sport. It was reserved for people who could afford long holidays and for those who had the necessary social education to seek a demanding and difficult leisure pursuit. One man changed all this and dominated the rock-climbing scene for more than a decade. During this period he raised the standard of technical rock climbing to a level unequalled anywhere in the world. That man was my father, Jim Birkett.

By the time Jim had recorded his first route, Tarsus (S) on Dove Crag, in 1937, he knew the mountains intimately. The name reflects his knowledge of birds, for a pigeon's shinbone, the Tarsus, lay on a ledge.

Born in Little Langdale on 26th April 1914, he was always a

natural. From a very early age he started collecting birds' eggs and soon developed a reputation as a lad who would 'climb out'. Come 'hay time', he would spend more time climbing the Lakeland slate barn walls than unloading the hay carts.

When Jim left school, at fourteen, he became an apprentice 'river' in a local slate quarry. A river is a man who splits large blocks of slate with a hammer and chisel. He soon developed phenomenal finger and arm strength, and this was to play a large part in many of his new routes. Shortly after leaving school he pushbiked to Glencoe, from Little Langdale, for 'nesting purposes', carrying, of course, all his gear on his back. This included his tent and the inevitable 'nesting rope', merely a farmer's cart rope.

Right from these early times Jim knew he was to be a climber. "As a lad I used to watch the climbers coming up Langdale on their motorbikes, ropes on their shoulders. They seemed to have a tremendous aura about them and I wanted to emulate them." It was around 1936 when Jim met Billy Jenkinson at the Honister quarries and found that they both felt the same way about rock climbing.

In the historical section of the 1936 Fell and Rock Climbing Club Scafell guidebook, C. F. Holland wrote, when talking of the East Buttress:

> The Girdle Traverse of this, our newest climbing ground, has yet to be made, and certainly there are other routes here to be added before long, while the wetness and ubiquitously vertical character of this region may well give it the right to challenge the present supremacy of Clogwyn D'ur Arddu, as the wettest, most dangerous and altogether the most formidable crag in the British Isles.

It was 1938 before Jim showed his true mettle with the ascent of May Day Climb (HVS) on the East Buttress. He had already ticked off all of Lakeland's hardest guidebook routes and, in all modesty, had found them easy. He was already highly proficient in nail and rope technique at this stage, due to his 'nesting' background, but on May Day, which he climbed with 'Chuck' Hudson and Charlie Wilson, he carried three pitons. Nobody really knew what to make of pitons at the time, and Jim was experimenting with a new and controversial aid to climbing. On the first pitch, which is technically 5c and was much harder than anything else yet climbed on the East Buttress, he belayed his second man to one piton on a ledge a little way up the first pitch, climbed the pitch unaided and put a piton for a belay at the ledge at the top. He did not in fact use this peg and traversed right to the end of the ledge and belayed on the remaining piton. (The pitons were placed by banging them in with a stone.) He never used pitons again. The Girdle of the East Buttress (HVS) followed in August of the same year.

It was Jim's first route in the following year, however, that caused a sensation. On All Fools' Day 1939 Overhanging Bastion (VS) fell. Hailed as a 'Lakeland Everest', it was a tremendous psychological breakthrough, following a beautiful natural line, up the centre of the Castle Rock of Triermain. Technically it was only VS but the psychological barrier had been tremendous and many considered this route to herald a new era. Bill Peascod had this to say: "Something started with Kelly after the first world war, but Overhanging Bastion was the start of a new era. It was most certainly the greatest climb of its time. Jim and myself were the last of a generation, by the fifties a new breed of climber had been born."

Zigzag (VS) again on Castle Rock, was done by the same team of Birkett, Wilson and Muscroft. Then a few weeks later Chuck Hudson fell off the Direct Start to Middlefell Buttress. Falling only a few feet, he broke his leg and ended up in Kendal Hospital. Jim was on his way to visit Chuck when, going flat out on his Ariel, he crashed into a cow at Clappersgate. A herd of cows being driven up the road were overtaken by the local vicar, on the wrong side of the road; Jim had almost negotiated the gap when a cow stuck its head out and clouted him on the thigh. Of course Jim was taken into Kendal Hospital and wheeled into the bed next to Chuck. Jim recalled the incident. He said, "I've come to see you, Chuck." Chuck replied, "You needn't have bothered like that." The season that had started so well and promised so much had come to an ignominious end, for Jim was immobile for the rest of the summer. He did, however, manage to get down to Clogwyn D'ur Arddu, while still signed off work. "We did Longlands, Great Slab and Narrow Slab and then burned back to the Lakes."

The following year, partnered notably by Vic Veevers, Jim put up North West Arete (MVS) on Gimmer, Eagle Cracks (VS) and Tophet Grooves (HVS); both on the Napes area of Great Gable.

They were good-quality routes, and Tophet Grooves was hard. They also showed Jim's diverse knowledge of the Lakeland crags. In three years he had now done eight new routes spread right across the Lakes, from Dove Crag in the east to Scafell in the west.

Arthur Dolphin, a great rock-climbing pioneer who over-lapped and succeeded Birkett, wrote of the second ascent of Tophet Grooves, which he did in 1947. The following account describes the ascent after two pitches, including the crux pitch, had been climbed:

> From the end of the ledge the rock fell away in one gigantic overhang split by a six inch wide crack. The continuation of this crack in the wall above led to familiar ground—a junction with the Tophet Girdle about fifty feet above our heads. Undercut at its base, the crack was wet and grassy and must have been a trying lead; a magnificent thread belay behind a massive block was the just reward, and, I received the word to follow. A shattered pinnacle seemed a useful take-off point for the awkward move into the crack. I was stepping up, pleased at having found an easy solution to the problem when, with a rumbling noise, the whole world seemed to fall apart and before I knew what had happened I was dangling on the rope. A loud crash signalled the arrival of the pinnacle on the screes. Somewhat shaken but otherwise undamaged, I started off again. This time I tested every hold. The grass in particular felt most unsatisfying!
>
> The final pitch, still by way of the crack, proved surprisingly resistant (perhaps a psychological reaction) and it was now beginning to get dark. I took an alternative route by way of Demon Wall. With the top rope Des then climbed the crack. It formed a fitting climax to a really first class route.

(Des Birch was his climbing partner.)

Through the inter-war years Jim kept climbing. 'F' Route on Gimmer Crag was notable, its main pitch being a superb seventy-five foot layback/jamming crack with the crux right at the top. Only two hundred feet of space lies beneath your feet. With modern protection it is a delight to climb; in 1941 it was a typically bold lead.

After the war sheer gold followed, culminating in Harlot Face (E1) which was the first Extreme climb in Britain. Jim had this to say: "Before the war I thought I could climb anything, afterwards I was past my best. I found Harlot Face hard, hence the name!"

The routes, however, speak for themselves. On Scafell Gremlin's Groove (VS) and South Chimney (HVS), both on the East Buttress, Square Chimney (VS), Esk Buttress, and the magnificent Slab and Groove (HVS), Scafell, stand out. I remember thinking when making the second ascent of Read and Adam's Lord of the Rings (E2)—this was the first continuous ascent—which starts up Gremlin's Groove, that if the flared crack of Gremlin's Groove was VS, then I might as well abseil off, for I stood no chance of climbing anything two full grades harder. (Lord of the Rings is a twelve-hundred-foot girdle of the East Buttress of Scafell. It remained unrepeated for six years.)

Although only short, Slab and Groove was a fitting culmination to Jim's exploration of Scafell. It gives two very contrasting pitches. The first wall is thin and was at the time unprotectable. It requires nerve and good technique. The groove requires a more physical approach but is straightforward and can be enjoyed.

In Langdale White Ghyll Wall (MVS), Slip Knotts (HVS), Haste Not (VS), Perhaps Not (HVS) and Do Not (HVS) are my favourites, and all successively opened up White Ghyll. White Ghyll is the epitome of a 'modern crag'. It is easily accessible (only ten minutes from the road) and grossly overhanging. The 'rock gymnast' can have a very full day here and still be gently introduced to the subtlety of the Lakeland Hills.

Actually Hollin Groove (S) was Jim's first route in the Ghyll and was climbed after a mysterious fire swept the Lower Crag free from its extensive vegetation. Quite an awkward start is followed by enjoyable climbing. Slip Knott and White Ghyll Wall are superb climbs in the lower grades. The holds are good but a reasonable level of commitment is required even with modern protection. Haste Not at VS has unbelievably spectacular positions and is to be recommended. Perhaps Not and Do Not are hard, and many people believe Do Not harder than Dolphin's superb Kipling Groove (HVS) of the same era. On Perhaps Not there is a very awkward chimney pitch. The Langdale guide says: "Faith in what may be above is required when the holds disappear." Jim's knowledge of the Lakeland rock helped here. He said: "The chimney was alright. It's only a few feet. I just pinched the rib, reached up to the right and there was a good hidden flake."

On Dow Crag, Leopard's Crawl was recorded as severe.

Immediately delicate and precarious, it now warrants Hard Very Severe. Even with modern equipment it can only be poorly protected—hence its elevated grade. Imagine climbing many of Jim's routes without protection; try on a pair of nailed boots, and the difference between then and present-day climbing standards may not seem too remote.

It was on the Eastern Fells, where Jim had started, that he closed down his new routing career. On Castle Rock, May Day Cracks (VS) gave a particularly steep and strenuous VS; often wet, it defeats many modern-day parties. Then in June 1949 came Harlot Face (E1) with Len Muscroft holding the rope, the hardest route in Britain at the time and undoubtedly, along with Overhanging Bastion, a breakthrough in climbing achievement. It was done on a Sunday only a week after putting up Do Not. In fact Jim's last route was done with Harry Griffen in 1954. Kestrel Wall on Eagle Crag, Griesdale, is HS and cannot be compared in difficulty with many of his other routes. It does, however, compare in quality, and this above all else can be said of Jim's routes: they are all excellent, irrespective of grade.

In all he recorded forty-eight new Lakeland routes. To follow Jim's routes through the Lakes is to follow a trail of good-quality routes of all grades on excellent rock. They combine beauty of movement with fine direction.

It has been said of Jim that he was the greatest exponent of nailed-boot climbing. When Jim started climbing with Billy Jenkinson, he went from nails to rubbers, because rubbers were the 'in' thing to climb in. He soon found, however, that rubbers were unsatisfactory in the wet. Those "black pumps from Woolworths" were popular but useless in the rain. So when he went back to climbing in nails, he had already considerable experience as he had been wearing them since he was fourteen. He climbed in tricouni clinkers and quarryman's clogs, but he preferred 'waisted' clinkers for Lake District rock.

When Jim had done all the hard routes of the day in rubbers, he went back and led them in nails. Remember in those days there was not the tremendous volume of routes there is now. The next stage was to descend the routes in nails. An example of this is the three eliminates on Dow Crag-Coniston, Eliminate A, Eliminate B and Eliminate C, all of which are 'worrying' VS. Jim led the first ascents in nails and was also the first to descend them in nails.

The thought of descending last man, in nails, down Eliminate B or reversing the crux of Eliminate C, which lies a hundred feet above the gully bed, sends a shudder down my spine.

To watch Jim in action with a pair of nails is to witness genius at work. He appears to float up apparently holdless rock with no effort whatsoever. The great attraction of nails is the absolutely minute rugosities that can be used if the boot is placed correctly. To complement this technique Jim used to shape his body in a curve, so transmitting all the weight ideally through his points of contact. Imagine a bird balancing on a clothes line, and this is the same principle. Of course, if boots are not placed correctly, then they will skid off, or if the rock strength is overestimated, then the rugosities break off. Using nails is a precise science which takes time and skill to learn. I do not think we will ever see their use again.

Transport to Jim meant motorbikes. The thrill of high-speed motorcycling was 'a must' for him. He owned and ran a succession of big, fast bikes in the days when British bikes were best: Cotton, Rudge, Velocettes, numerous Nortons including the Norton 'International', BSA and probably his favourite the Ariel, culminating in the Twin Port Ariel Red Hunter. I remember that he fitted a side-car to the Red Hunter, and it provided family transport for fifteen years. Great days of sitting on the petrol tank with Dad sliding it round the bends, cloth cap with the peak pointing backwards.

Descending down from Honister Pass into Borrowdale, just past the Seathwaite road end, there is a hump-backed bridge followed by a row of cottages. Jim always reckoned he could 'take off' at the bridge and land at the fifth cottage on his Norton. Indisputably 'Dare Devil', it requires skill and courage, although many would regard it as irresponsible.

Irresponsible Jim never was when climbing. He has never once fallen off or climbed anything he could not reverse. Always climbing within his limits, he still managed to push up climbing standards. Natural ability Jim certainly had, but this was combined with total dedication and training. Not only did he have an extremely physical job but winter evenings were spent at the gymnasium, and along with Chuck Hudson and Charlie Wilson he combined gymnastics with weightlifting. He also spent hours bouldering, and really most evenings during the summer Jim was on the Fells until dark.

I was on the verge of the common man entering the annals of the sport. Climbers are no better now, or worse. Men have always been sorted out from the boys. Botterill, Herford, Sansom—that type has always been there and is still with us today, but I will say in Botterill's day they didn't know what was possible, today they do. There will always be real climbers though. Every sport has its naturals—with application and dedication they become superstars.

One, often quoted, Jim Birkett phrase is: "If I get my fingers over something, the rest will generally follow," but he has retreated from a number of potential new climbs because he thought it dangerous to continue with the techniques then available. Whillan's 1960 route up the centre of Dove is one such line. Eastern Hammer (Livesey, E3, 1974) and Poacher (Austin, E1, 1963) are others. One outstanding 'failure' was when he climbed up the White Cone on Castle Rock, failed to get up the groove above and traversed left onto the easy slabs extending from Zigzag. This of course climbed the crux of Rigor Mortis E2 long before Paul Ross chipped his way across in 1959.

His climbing activities extended beyond rock, and he visited the Alps and Norway on a number of occasions. He notched up some very quick ascents in Norway, doing a two-day mixed route in a number of hours, and this apparently became front-page news in the local paper. He climbed snow and ice in Scotland and the Lakes, although he was never fond of Lakes winter climbing—"cold and nasty". He did, however, two outstanding Lakes winter ascents wearing tricounis and sporting a single long ice-axe. One was inaccessible Gully IV, on Dove Crag, which I personally find very hard indeed with all the modern gear, i.e. front-point crampons and two terradactyles, ice screws and rock peg protection! The other was Engineer's Chimney IV/V, where Len Muscroft reckoned he had never seen Jim so committed. "He moved out from the gully across the wall on verglas and cleared his throat." On the rare occasions Jim found something hard, he would involuntarily clear his throat with a short rasping cough, a purely nervous reaction. "When he did this I knew it was going to be desperate." (Engineer's Chimney had been climbed some time previously for the first time in winter by Jack Carswell.)

Len Muscroft was most probably Jim's favourite rock-climbing partner. Occasionally leading, he could always be depended on to follow the most difficult of pitches. Jim said: "I always felt I could climb anything with Len holding the rope."

Coolness, steadiness and mental courage were the main requirements of a second man, especially when Jim Birkett was leading. Perhaps Not (HVS), on White Ghyll-Langdale, is a good illustration. After a long, serious and exposed traverse following an undercut ramp below the main overhangs, one arrives at the stance, a rock ledge a mere eight inches wide, where it is impossible to stand in balance due to the bulging nature of the rock. Here Len was belayed, hanging from the exposed root of a sapling, a mere half inch in diameter, which had fought to live in some cracks beneath the overhang.

Jim proceeded to lead the crux chimney (5b), climbing on light Alpine line (hemp) with no further protection, while all the time Len hung, smiling no doubt, from his pathetic and purely symbolic belay. This was undoubtedly one of Britain's hardest routes at that time, and the stance is now, tragically, bristling with pegs. I once asked Jim what they belayed on; in his usual fashion he looked the other way and very quietly muttered, "Oh we had a tree or something."

Of course it was with Len that he climbed many of his major routes, culminating in Do Not (HVS) and Harlot Face (E1), done on successive weekends. I often wonder if they consider they were cheating on Harlot Face. Indeed it must have been a very relaxing day out for Len. After all, they had a belay and a ledge to stand on half way up the route.

Fortunately Len was not without a sense of humour, as the following ditty, written by him, shows:

My Choice

> Some may sigh for airy heights
> With slabs all sleek and greasy,
> And holdless walls with overhangs
> To traverse not so easy,
> But give me a chimney, brother,
> Despite its dirt and slime,
> Where I can thrust my back and foot
> And wriggle up the climb.

The flora and fauna of the mountains has always been Jim's

main interest. 'Nesting', the stealing of eggs, was replaced by protecting them, marking the eggs with indelible ink, which makes them valueless to collectors, and he was issued a licence by the Nature Conservancy to carry out this service. His specialist knowledge of plant habitat and mountain bird life is often drawn upon by university specialists.

Jim has always had his 'hairiest' moments while nesting. His abseiling exploits have to be seen to be believed. He jumps, swings and runs and seems to be able to reach any part of the cliff to examine a bird's nest or some rare plant. He often uses tension belays which are just slings held on to the rock edges or flakes by the tension of the abseil rope—as soon as the weight comes off the rope, the belay springs off (very good for leaving an area quickly but leaving no margin for error). He also uses an abseil bar, of light alloy, which he places in the thin soil above a crag. On one such occasion the bar went in half an inch, and Jim had his nesting companion, a non-climber, sit on the bar to hold it *in situ*. The man refused, claiming it was suicide, but when Jim started down anyway, he flung himself over the bar, and the static dead load was sufficient to hold it secure. Unfortunately, the incident rather shattered the confidence of the companion, and he refused to go out with Jim again.

Looking for plants and nesting entailed much soloing and many's the time I have been unable to follow the 'old man'— usually through fear but occasionally because I have found it physically impossible. His worst moment came on the three-hundred-foot-high cliffs of St Bees. He had soloed across Lawson's Leap, a distance of about twenty feet, to a partially detached sandstone pinnacle. He returned via a sliver of sandstone jammed across the gap. When half way across, he was standing upright, walking 'tightrope' fashion, and the soft sandstone ends crumbled and the sliver rotated. Jim maintained his balance, and the rock held. "It was the only time a situation has been beyond my control. I just accepted it. I really thought that was the end."

In his younger days Jim was a hard, totally uncompromising man of immense physical strength and fitness, qualities that saw him pioneer the hardest routes and brought him from 'river' to foreman and then manager of a Lakeland slate quarry, a position which he holds to this day. Often asked by my mother why he did not apply his specialist knowledge commercially, he would just shake his head. A thoroughly modest man, he detests fuss and avoids publicity. To work among slate, the rock of Lakeland, and to have the privilege and freedom of the hills is Jim's ultimate experience.

Route name	Grade	Location	Comments
1937 The Tarsus	HS	Dove Crag	
1938 May Day Climb	HVS	East Buttress, Scafell	Hardest route in Britain at the time. Climbed on 1st May
1938 East Buttress Girdle	HVS	East Buttress, Scafell	
1939 Overhanging Bastion	HVS	Castle Rock	A major break-through in concept. Climbed on All Fools' Day, 1st April
1939 Zigzag	VS	Castle Rock	
1939 The Gossard	VS	Castle Rock	Gossard, the best girdle
1940 Eagle Cracks	VS	The Napes, Great Gable	
North Wall	VS	A Buttress, Dow Crag	
North West Arete	MVS	Gimmer Crag, Langdale	
Tophet Grooves	HVS	Tophet Bastion, Great Gable	
1941 F Route	VS	Gimmer Crag	
Bachelor Crack	HS	Gimmer Crag	
1944 Esk Buttress Girdle	VS	Esk Buttress, Scafell	
Serpent Route	HS	Esk Buttress, Scafell	
Afterthought	S	Esk Buttress, Scafell	
Frustration	HS	Esk Buttress, Scafell	
Chimney Buttress	VD	Esk Buttress, Scafell	
Cinderella	MVS	Blind Tarn Crag, Dow	
1945 Great Central Climb	VS	Esk Buttress, Scafell	
Steep Ghyll Grooves	MVS	Scafell—Pisgah Buttress	
Gremlin's Grooves	HVS	East Buttress, Scafell	
South Chimney	HVS	East Buttress, Scafell	
Gargoyle Stair	HS	East Buttress, Scafell	
Thor's Cave	MS	East Buttress, Scafell	
Thunder Rib	VD	East Buttress, Scafell	
1945 Hollin's Groove	S	White Ghyll, Langdale	

	Route name	*Grade*	*Location*	*Comments*
1946	White Ghyll Wall	MVS	White Ghyll, Langdale	
	White Ghyll Traverse	VS	White Ghyll, Langdale	
1947	Slip Knot	MVS	White Ghyll, Langdale	
	Junction Arete	VD	White Ghyll, Langdale	Len Muscroft led
	Heather Groove	VD	White Ghyll, Langdale	
	May Day Cracks	VS	Castle Rock	Climbed on May 1st
	Castle Wall	MVS	Castle Rock	
	Flying Buttress	VS	Castle Rock	
	Chapel Cracks	MVS	Castle Rock	
	Square Chimney	VS	Esk Buttress	
	Leopard's Crawl	HVS	B Buttress, Dow Crag	Thought to be Severe by Jim!
	Eliminate B— Direct Start	HVS	B Buttress, Dow Crag	
1948	Haste Not	VS	White Ghyll	
	Poker's Parade	HS	White Ghyll	
	Granny Knot	HS	White Ghyll	
	Raven's Groove	MVS	Gillercombe, Borrowdale	Len Muscroft led
	Slab & Groove	HVS	Scafell	
1949	Why Not	HVD	White Ghyll, Langdale	
	Perhaps Not	HVS	White Ghyll, Langdale	
	Do Not	HVS	White Ghyll, Langdale	
	Harlot Face	E1	Castle Rock	The first Extreme—the hardest climb in Britain
1954	Kestrel Wall	HS	Eagle Crag, Griesdale	

9

Bill Peascod
(3rd May 1920–   )

It takes a man with a special kind of dedication to climb in an unpopular area, on cliffs that are large and serious due to their remoteness, looseness and vegetation. Bill Peascod was such a man.

Hailing from West Cumberland, he became known for his development of the north-western fells. Previously untouched and relatively unknown there lay hidden, in this the most beautiful part of Lakeland, some large and major crags. He became respected for his bold and unprotected leads, his physical strength and his depth of personality. Naturally strong, he started work at the coal face and developed his physical strength even further by a dedicated programme of weight training. As for his personality, he is a rare man, being both a chartered mining engineer and an internationally renowned artist. Leaving Britain in 1952 he began a new life in Australia and inevitably pioneered a number of routes over there. Recently he returned to the Lake District and intends to open an arts/adventure centre near

Bassenthwaite. I have little doubt it will succeed.

Bill was born in industrial West Cumberland, in the town of Maryport, on 3rd May 1920. Living in Workington when a schoolboy, he remembers frequenting the library virtually every day, withdrawing a book, reading it and returning it the same day. He was an avid young reader. It was here, reading O. G. Jones's marvellous book *Rock Climbing in the English Lake District* and the Abraham publications, that he was given the incentive to take up rock climbing for himself.

He started work in the West Cumbrian coal pits at the age of fourteen, where hard work produced stamina and physical strength. At the age of sixteen he was walking into the Lakes, and the magic of his local Cumberland Fells enchanted him. These were "good walks". Starting from Workington he would walk to Grassmoor via Loweswater, climb Lorton Gully to the summit of Grassmoor and return to Workington in the same day. Buttermere seemed to have an irresistible draw for Bill, and he would visit there and return via Ennerdale to his home in Workington. There were good thirty-mile trips, involving many miles of ascents and descents.

Scrambling led to climbing, and he remembers soloing gullies, optimistically trailing a fifty-foot rope behind him, hoping it would 'catch' if he fell off.

Struggling to find companions on these outings, he remembers just how incompatible climbing and living in a local mining community were. Believe it or not, and I can confirm this whole-heartedly—being born and bred in Little Langdale—locals regarded venturing onto the hills as an oddity and just "bliddy daft", so Bill would hide his climbing rope at the bottom of his rucksack. It was returning from one of his marathon walks and some three miles outside Workington that he was passed by a bus containing the local Rambling Club. The bus stopped, and from then on Bill was not without people of like mind.

He remembers one of his first climbs to be Stack Ghyll (HS) on the Haystacks-Buttermere, and in this horrendously loose route his fingers were smashed by a falling boulder. Laid off work, he was in no way deterred; in fact his appetite for Buttermere climbing became insatiable. Later, on Haystacks with S. B. Beck, he pioneered Y Gully (VS), a frightening piece of climbing. Ray McHaffie made the second ascent of the Gully and the first

North West Arete, Gimmer Crag, first climbed by Jim
Birkett in 1940.

From left to right: A. T. Hargreaves, Ruth Hargreaves, 'Jammy' Cross and John Heap. [The Knee belongs to Sid Cross]

A. T. Hargreaves.

Castle Rock of Triermain, first ascended by the great curving ramp up the centre by Jim Birkett on 1st April 1939 and called Overhanging Bastion.

(*top left*)
Slab and Groove,
Scafell, first climbed by
Jim Birkett, without any
protection, in 1948.

(*above*)
Jim Birkett belaying
above Gimmer Crag,
1934.

Jim Birkett belayed by
Charlie Wilson on Kern
Knotts, Great Gable.

(*top left*) Bill Peascod in Australia.

(*top right*) Bill Peascod with Bert Beck on the first ascent of Dexter Wall (VS), on Grey Crag, Buttermere, March 1941.

(*bottom left*) Bill Peascod leading the first ascent of Resurrection Route (VS), High Crag, Buttermere, in the rain in September 1941.

(*bottom right*) Bill Peascod's great 'roadside classic' climb, Cleopatra (HVS, 1951) on Buckstone Howe, Honister.

(*opposite*) Arthur Dolphin on the first ascent of Kipling Groove, Gimmer Crag, Whitsuntide 1948.

(*bottom left*) Arthur Dolphin at Ilkley Quarry.

(*bottom right*) Deer Bield Crag, Easdale. The climber is on Arthur Dolphin's Deer Bield Buttress, one of the first climbs to be graded Extreme (1951). Above and left is a great black pod, and this is the line of the 'horrendous' Deer Bield Crack (HVS) climbed by A. T. Hargreaves in 1930.

Alan Austin at Raw Head, Langdale.

Pete Livesey, rock athlete.

Early days: Pete Livesey on Central Pillar, Esk Buttress.

Rod Valentine on Pete Livesey's Bitter Oasis (E3, 1974), on Goat Crag, Borrowdale, a brilliant route typifying the ferocity of modern rock climbing.

winter ascent—he reckoned it was easier in winter! Summer ascents can be counted on the fingers of one hand. S. B. Beck told me that he thought at the time that, if he was lucky enough to get out of the Gully alive (he did not think he would), he would never climb again. Of course he did and accompanied Bill on many more first ascents.

Bill's Lakeland pioneering activities began with a couple of rather minor sorties on Round Howe, a delightfully remote and compact little crag lying at the extreme head of the Buttermere Valley. Chimney Route (VD) and Central Route (MS) were done in 1939 and 1940 respectively.

Young and fearless, his next new route was very different: in 1940 he tackled the big dank and impressive Eagle Crag. Eagle towers over Birkness Combe on the west side of the Buttermere Valley. It is a major crag, some five hundred feet high, and is comparable with the best in the Lakes.'Far East Buttress' was the route. It is graded VS and is at the top of this grade.

Until this event Eagle had remained remote, almost unnoticed by the busy climbing world of Langdale and Wasdale. It is true that Piggot had first breached Eagle's defences in April 1925, providing a route he named Western Buttress Ordinary (HS), and Cross, with Kelly and party, had produced routes, notably Double Cross Routes (VS), 1937, but these climbs did not have the same purposefulness of line.

The following week Border Buttress (HS) and 'Eagle Girdle' (VS) were put up. Then on 23rd June one of Lakeland's great routes was produced. 'Eagle Front' (VS), five hundred feet, forced its way up the main buttress. It was the best and hardest climb in Buttermere at that time, and it remains a superb climb today.

Only four weeks later Peascod was back again, accompanied, as on the preceding climb, by S. B. Beck. They climbed the main buttress again by a very serious route named 'Fifth Avenue' (320 feet). It is graded VS in the guide but I think HVS is the more appropriate grade. The crux pitch involves a 150-foot run-out of rope; it is hard, and the holds are sloping, a thoroughly frightening piece of climbing. When Bill led it, he was climbing into the unknown, with no protection and on belays that were hopelessly inadequate. This was certainly one of the most impressive Lake District leads. He was only twenty years old at the time, and many fruitful years lay ahead.

After Eagle Crag, Bill turned his attention to the nearby Grey Crag, with sorties onto High Crag, the massive Haystacks, and Yew Crag—all in his beloved Buttermere Valley. Then in 1946 he started the development of Buckstone Howe with the notable 'Sinister Grooves' (VS). This crag is impressively situated among the slate works above Honister Pass. It dries quickly and can be reached in ten minutes' easy walk from the road. The rock is slate, the crag being surrounded with a fascinating tapestry of industrial archaeology, and requires cunning and careful ue. It is a fitting crag for a mining engineer to develop. The crag and the climb are so good that it is almost inconceivable that it had been by-passed by all previous climbers. Jim Birkett, a quarryman, lived (the youth hostel used to accommodate the quarry workman in the 1940s) and worked at Honister for a number of years, yet he never even looked at Buckstone Howe!

Groove Two (VS) followed, and this was a technical master-piece. Many present-day leaders fail to enter the final groove. I rate it at least 5A technically, and these days, although protectable with micro nuts, it is still a demanding lead. In 1951, Cleopatra (VS) was forced; again the VS grade seems inappropriate—I would certainly give it an HVS grade. The climb itself is just excellent and has been described as the first modern roadside classic climb. A classic route is one, whatever its grade, that can be chosen from an era and represents all that is best about that era. The designation 'classic' guarantees that the route will be of high quality and will be enjoyable—like a good piece of music or a twelve-year-old bottle of malt whisky. Cleopatra is superb: it gives technical and challenging climbing on tight slate.

Another impressive and major crag was opened up by Peascod in 1946. This was again called Eagle Crag, but this crag is situated above Langstrath in Borrowdale. The month was June and in the space of two weeks Falconer's Crack (VS), the Great Stair (MVS) and Postern Gate (HS) were climbed. Almost unbelievably, again from a crag unclimbed on before, Peascod produced three excellent climbs of their grade. Falconer's Crack remains the classic of the crag.

I remember a few years ago (I was fifteen at the time), I was attempting Falconer's Crack with a reasonably experienced climber who was twenty. This lad had led Extreme climbs in Wales, and he was somewhat of a hero figure to me. We reached the third pitch, and he started off to lead it. He pulled up a groove and then round a rib on the left to gain a wall. It seemed extremely steep, and he could find no protection. After much trying he conceded defeat, returned to the belay and announced we should abseil off. Fascinated by the pitch, I refused, took over the lead and climbed the pitch and the one above. It was a wonderful climbing, steep and technical, with little or no protection and tremendously exposed. I will always remember that unique feeling of fear and exhilaration. For me it was a great climb, and there are few I have enjoyed more.

In 1948 Bill returned to Buttermere to climb the rather awesome 'Central Chimney' (VS) on Eagle Crag. It has been the obvious line from the start, a deep cut cleft in the centre of the crag. Starting off quite meekly, it suddenly changes character, and the final two hundred feet are most intimidating. The chimney had seen many attempts: in 1907 the rock-climbing genius of Fred Botterill had been turned back, and in 1918 H. Raeburn and H. Binns were defeated. The chimney was, however, no match for Bill Peascod in his prime.

In 1949 Bill wrote an excellent article entitled 'The Cinderella of Climbing Valleys', referring of course to his beloved Buttermere. In this article he described the first ascent of his routes including the Central Chimney: "We were now in a large, overhanging, cleft with a narrow exit between the overhang and the right wall. The exit, guarded as it was by an intimidating bulge, proved to be one of the most awkward sections of the climb. This pitch is also an anxious one for the leader because of tricky landing, and an ascent of rounded slabs to a corner. The pitch is 80 foot long and the belay is reached thankfully." Bill finished the article: "Buttermere has been described as a Cinderella among climbing centres. I believe she can now be said to be wearing the Glass Slipper."

In the same year Bill focused his attention on the Newlands Valley, and in August, with George Rushworth, he climbed the notable Dale Head Pillar (MVS). Peascod's activities in Newlands ended in 1951 with his ascent of Jezebel (VS), climbed with Stan Dirkin. It is interesting to know that on the same day they produced a left-to-right girdle traverse, graded VS and quite distinguished. It was never written up in the FRCC guidebook, and it still awaits a second ascent some thirty years later.

Delilah (MVS) on High Crag was climbed in 1951 and was Peascod's last new climb before he departed for Australia. He left behind a legacy of over fifty climbs, and some of these were truly great.

Ironically, Bill's worst climb bears his name. On Far East Raven Crag in Langdale, climbing on unfamiliar ground, he put up an undistinguished route. He refused to name it and did not record it. Perhaps mischievously, Arthur Dolphin found out about the climb and wrote it up in the Langdale guide. Because it had no name attached to it, he called it Peascod's Route—Arthur loved irony.

Very fortuitously I have recently had the great pleasure of meeting Bill Peascod and not only discussing his climbs but actually climbing with him. To my surprise and admiration he had no trouble at all doing Lakeland VS climbs after thirty years' absence. He climbed Eve (MVS) on Shepherd's Crag in Borrowdale, a climb of which he had made the first ascent almost exactly thirty years earlier and where he did at least five routes on a very cold February day. Watching him bridge delicately, precisely and quickly up a VS corner crack, it was if he had never been away.

In 1946 and 1947 Bill was deeply affected by two mining disasters due to underground explosions. First the No. 10 pit at Lowca saw fifteen men killed, and a year later at Whitehaven 104 men were lost. Involved in rescue operations, he became determined to leave the pits while he still had the option.

During the war years Bill worked at college and his labours bore fruit when eventually he became a chartered engineer (mining), and he left the pits to teach mining at Workington Technical College. But by 1952 he had had enough of struggling to earn a reasonable living from teaching, and he departed for Australia. Climbing, of course, did not cease, and he pioneered many new routes in the then completely virgin ranges. Based in New South Wales, notable new ascents included the Bread Knife in the Warrumbungles in 1954. And others followed, in the Glasshouse Mountains, particularly on the seventeen-hundred-foot-high pyramid-shaped Beerwah, a spectacular spike of undesite rising from the flat of the surrounding plains.

Australia saw his talents as an artist blossom and bear fruit. The seeds sown at art college, which he had attended for only a short time in distant Workington, had at last matured. Exhibition followed exhibition, and his work is now internationally recognized.

Talking to Bill, I found it interesting how his climbing philosophy and attitude had developed. In the early days Bill was fearless, putting up major routes, Eagle Front and the like, in his first year of real climbing. No protection, loose rock and hard climbing all felt very good, and his enthusiasm was limitless. He reckons that good climbers are born good and that if you are going to climb well, then you will do so immediately. Every day of every weekend was spent climbing both summer and winter.

Enthusiasm was, however, tempered with bitter experience. One morning in Brackenclose, a young man, D. M. K. Horn, eighteen years old, was alone and wanting someone to climb with. He was ignored. Later, on Pillar, Bill with S. B. Beck was descending across the top of Walker's Gully after doing the south-west route. They heard a flapping noise, like a crow exiting from a tight crack, but not quite. Bill, always eager, was at the bottom of Grooved Wall first, ready for another climb, when he discovered the body of Horn, who had fallen while soloing North Climb. Afterwards he realized the danger of falling, and this in fact had a steadying influence. "I was lightweight in experience so I got a pair of nailed boots and learned to use them." He most certainly did that, and the first ascent of Resurrection Route (VS) on High Crag and a repeat ascent of Grooved Wall were both done in nails and in the rain, shortly afterwards.

His confidence in rock climbing returned, and weightlifting provided the necessary physical strength required when he left the pits for a lecturing post. When he had been working at the coal face, he would finish on night shift and go straight out climbing, often pushbiking to the Lakes on a Saturday morning and climbing all weekend. He never, however, climbed weekdays after work. This was true even after he had taken up teaching, although there was enough time to do so. It seemed that certain conventions of West Cumberland Society were hard to break.

Apart from his Lakeland activities Bill was active in Scotland and with G. G. Macphee did early ascents of Rubicon Wall (VS) and Long Climb (VS), both on Ben Nevis. They also climbed Clachaig Gully (VS) in Glencoe in four hours, the previous best being seven hours. Bill went on to do two first ascents on Ben Nevis. These were Minus Two Gully (VS) and No. 5 Gully

Buttress (VS), both with B. L. Dodson. His Welsh visits were less frequent, and he took an impressive fall off Soap Gut (in the pouring rain), only saved by virtue of his rope jamming alongside a small chockstone! No runners, you see.

The wet summer of 1950 saw Bill, along with Brian Dodson, experimenting with a climbing harness they had devised, known as the 'Gatesgarth Sling'. Bill wore it from then on. It is not unlike the fully body harness favoured by many Continental climbers today and was designed to distribute the load in the event of a fall.

Bill has some fond recollections of the climbing scene in the forties. He regards the period as a very important bridge between Very Severe and Extreme climbing. There was, of course, friendly competition but this was good-natured. He remembers doing the Girdle Traverse on Eagle Crag, Buttermere, which on the right-hand side links the Double Cross and Half Nelson climbs about half way up. He believes that the route that Sid Cross meant to climb was up the lower part of Half Nelson, across the line of the Girdle, and then up the groove of Double Cross to finish, so making a very good route. They presumably could not climb the link pitch, the line of the Girdle. Bill remembers his mischievous thrill of satisfaction when A. T. Hargreaves closely questioned him on this section of the Girdle.

There was friendship too, and he remembers how alone in the Brackenclose hut in the 1930s A. T. Hargreaves and his wife Ruth befriended him and took him climbing. Also the Thompson brothers, if they passed you on the road, would flag your car down and stop their own and jump out. They would then immediately relate what they had climbed the preceding weekend, what they were about that weekend and what they intended for the following weekend. They would then jump into their car and head for the hills.

Bill also remembers that some routes went many years without second ascents. Such a route was Buttonhook Route (HVS) on Kern Knotts. Having watched Jim Birkett float up it and making the delicate traverse appear to be covered in jugs, it took Bill three attempts to make the third ascent because he could not get anybody to second the first pitch.

On his own Eagle Front, he returned to do the second ascent eight years after he had initially led it. "Walking through the farmyard at Gatesgarth I picked up a rusty four inch nail and put it in my pocket. I banged it in to a belay on at the end of pitch five—I wasn't going to do it without a belay this time!" There is, unfortunately, a piton in place these days.

Bill wrote of the Crux pitch:

> The view of the Coombe below is interrupted by neither rock nor grass. The Wall above and to the left may be written off; only to the right does the way seem feasible, and on this ascent the traverse, across a Water Worn Slab on rounded holds, became increasingly "interesting" when a film of water made its presence felt on rubber soled footwear. When one gets into such a position the second none too happily placed, the ground a long way below, and progress in any direction only possible by movements which are attended by 'natural hazards' I think a climber must cease to regard himself as a member of a party, welded together by three strong strands of rope, and climb with the intensity and concentration of a man going solo on similar rocks. And so it was here. The final crack led joyfully to the easier summit rocks and we had made the second ascent to Eagle Front.

Also on Ben Nevis on the first ascent of Minus Two Gully, G. G. MacPhee was belayed on the ground and was hit by a falling rock dislodged by Bill. Covered in blood Macphee announced he would retire to the hut and off he walked. "I thought I'd killed him," Bill said, "until he just walked off."

So that is the man Bill Peascod, one of Lakeland's greatest pioneers. I asked him what led him to climb so extensively in the north-western Fells, and he replied that the potential of his local crags was vast and that really there was no need to look further for new routes. "Doing new routes is like a disease. It possesses you, and you don't want to stop." His one regret was not doing the first ascent of High Crag Buttress (HVS), for after spending all day on the route he had failed to lead the awkward move at the top. Time ran out and Bill went to Australia. It was subsequently climbed in 1963 by another party, but they succeeded only by using pitons for aid.

After climbing with Bill Peascod, I came to the conclusion that there is no substitute for ability. In his own words, "Good climbers are born good." I would like to add, "Once a natural always a natural."

As Bill drove me into Keswick along the Bassenthwaite Road, the sun was just setting over Cat Bells and Causey Pike. It was October, the autumn colours had arrived, and a velvet glow hung in the sky. "You know, there's nowhere more beautiful than the Lakes," he said.

	Route name	Grade	Location
1939	Chimney Route	VD	Round Howe, Buttermere
1940	Central Route	MVS	Round Howe, Buttermere
	Far East Buttress	VS	Eagle Crag, Buttermere
	Border Buttress	HS	Eagle Crag, Buttermere
	Eagle Girdle	VS	Eagle Crag, Buttermere
	Eagle Front	VS	Eagle Crag, Buttermere
	Fifth Avenue	VS	Eagle Crag, Buttermere
1941	Dexter Wall	VS	Grey Crag, Buttermere
	The Y Gully	VS	Grey Crag, Buttermere
	Suaviter	MS	Grey Crag, Buttermere
	Fortiter	MVS	Grey Crag, Buttermere
	Resurrection Route	VS	High Crag, Buttermere
	Rowan Route	S	High Crag, Buttermere
	Flake & Crack	S	High Crag, Buttermere
	Holly Tree Groove	HS	Yew Crag, Buttermere
	Yew Crag Chimney	VD	Yew Crag, Buttermere
1942	Brant Bield Buttress		Birkness Coombe, Buttermere
	Harrow Wall	VD	Grey Crag, Buttermere
	Slabs West Route	HS	Grey Crag, Buttermere
	Haskett Buttress—		
	East Buttress Pillar	S	Haskett Buttress—Pillar Area
1943	Raven Crack	HVD	Grey Crag, Buttermere
1945	Wriggling Route—	VS	Pike's Crag, Scafell
	Spider Wall	MVS	Grey Crag, Buttermere
	Rib and Wall	D	Grey Crag, Buttermere
	Long Tom	HS	Grey Crag, Buttermere
	Peascod's Route	MVS	Far East, Raven Crag, Langdale
1946	Sinister Grooves	VS	Buckstone Howe
	Honister Wall	HS	Buckstone Howe
	Falconer's Crack	VS	Eagle Crag, Borrowdale
	The Great Stair	MVS	Eagle Crag, Borrowdale
1946	Postern Gate	HS	Eagle Crag, Borrowdale
1947	Groove One	VD	Buckstone Howe, Buttermere
	Groove Two	VS	Buckstone Howe, Buttermere
1948	Buckstone Girdle	VS	Buckstone Howe, Buttermere
	Tail Gate	VD	Eagle Crag
	Newland's Buttress	S	Miner's Crag, Newlands
	Double Slab	VD	Miner's Crag, Newlands
	Corkscrew	HS	Miner's Crag, Newlands
	Central Chimney	VS	Eagle Crag
	Waterfall Buttress		
	(Direct Route)	MS	Waterfall Buttress, Newlands
	Miner's Grooves	MVS	Miner's Crag, Newlands
	Alcove Ridge	S	Grey Buttress, Newlands
	Cossack Crack	VS	Red Crag
	Dale Head Pillar	MVS	Dale Head Crag

Route name	Grade	Location
1950 Black Crag Route	S	Pillar Area
1950 Hailstorm	HS	Long Crag, Bowness Knott, Ennerdale
1951 Cleopatra	VS	Buckstone Howe
1951 Jezebel	VS	Miner's Crag, Newlands
1951 Girdle Traverse	VS	Miner's Crag, Newlands
1951 Eve	MVS	Shepherds Crag, Borrowdale
Delilah	MVS	High Crag, Buttermere

10

Arthur Rhodes Dolphin
(15th March 1925–25th July 1953)

When I was at school, we had a teacher who seemingly knew a parable for every facet of human existence. His favourite was the tale of the rose tree: the harder one cut back its branches, the better it flourished—the greater the personal tragedy, the better one would become.

The summer of his life was short, yet to the few that knew him and to the many who only know of his climbs, the white rose that was Arthur Dolphin is acknowledged as Yorkshire's finest. This figure, surrounded by tragedy and whose family background and death are cruelly sad, rose like a phoenix from the ashes to become the greatest and most popular climber of his generation.

This modest, most shy, frail-looking, academically brilliant man took over from Birkett to pioneer Lakeland's hardest rock climbs. Consolidating the Extreme grade, he pushed standards higher than ever before with such routes as Kipling Groove (HVS), 1948, Rubicon Groove (HVS), 1951, Deer Bield Buttress (E1), 1951, Sword of Damocles (E1), 1952 and Hell's Groove

(E1), 1952. The first of a new generation, he was certainly using more advanced protection techniques than Birkett, yet he missed the real advances in equipment and was the last of the great unprotected leaders. It was said that Birkett would use only one sling (running belay) for protection in every hundred feet of climbing whereas Arthur would use five! Today, on the hardest routes, it is not uncommon to have five runners every ten feet.

Jim Birkett, a man who does not mince words and whose praise is earned only by great deeds, said of Dolphin: "Arthur was a super bloke. I liked him a lot. He was one of the best. I admired him because he was dead straight, never sponged. Entirely self-reliant, he travelled by motor bike and of course in the earlier days he pushbiked. He was the most unlikely looking climber ever, long, thin and anaemic. He always had a drip at the end of his nose. But could he climb!"

At a very early age Arthur began to shine as an outstanding rock climber. He started because his parents encouraged their rather sickly offspring to walk on the nearby Ilkley and Shipley Moors. Walking developed into scrambling on the gritstone outcrops and quarries. It was regarded as a good form of therapy for this ghost-like youth, son of a sporting Yorkshire family. Soon he was cycling, accompanied by his school friends, further afield, to the bigger gritstone edges—notably Almscliffe.

Development was rapid, from early scrambling to making Almscliffe his own crag. (It is said by many to be so called because the crag is very hard and strenuous and all the climbing is done on the arms. Arthur would have liked this weak pun.) The move to the bigger Lakeland cliffs did not take long. One of his first Lakeland leads was the Girdle Traverse on Dow Crag, a thousand feet long and a serious route which was then at the top of the grade, Very Severe. To reach this imposing challenge Arthur took the train from Leeds to Windermere and then cycled from Windermere station to Coniston, some twenty miles, followed by a two-hour walk. He was fourteen years old.

Arthur was born at Low Baildon near Bradford. His father was a grocer, and the family (he had both a sister and a brother) were comfortably off but simple-living and unpretentious. While at Salts Grammar School Arthur's brother, although too shy to play in an organized game of cricket, was a talented spin bowler who apparently tutored Jim Laker! Their uncle, also Arthur Dolphin, was one of England's finest 'stumpers', a wicket-keeper who played for both Yorkshire and England.

Following his brother, Arthur also attended Salts Grammar School, and he shone both academically and physically. Not only was he climbing intensively, and this was always his first love, but he represented his school and Yorkshire at cross-country running. After school he had intended to pursue a pure science degree, preferably in physics, but the war intervened, and he was sent to do metallurgy rather than serve in the forces. He gained a BSc at Leeds University.

At the outbreak of war his father was already a cripple, and during the war years his mother died and his brother was lost whilst serving in the RAF. By the start of the 1950s only Arthur and his sister remained from this once happy and prosperous family.

His early climbing days were spent chiefly on the local gritstone outcrops. At thirteen years of age he was leading his schoolfriends up the hardest gritstone routes, literally using his mother's washing line to protect their upward progress. He climbed in shoes, pumps, hobnailed boots, any damn thing really! Lack of basic equipment meant very little to Arthur for his determination to get at the rock and climb was absolute. His enthusiasm alone swept all other obstacles aside.

The early war years restricted movement, and Arthur was forced to concentrate his immense skill and effort solely on the local grit outcrops for Wales, Scotland and the Lakes were out of bounds to this determined schoolboy. Consequently Almscliffe, Ilkley, Widdop and many more grit outcrops all took a pounding from Arthur, particularly Almscliffe, where C. Frankland had made a series of very hard climbs taking the more obvious and feasible-looking lines. Frankland ensured that any new climbs that remained to be done would be of a new and higher standard of difficulty.

In 1940 Arthur rose to the challenge with a series of gritstone routes that are all very hard and very good. In his first year of new routing he put up such classic grit routes as Demon Wall (VS), Overhanging Groove (VS), Black Wall (VS) and Z Climb (VS), to take but one crag, Almscliffe naturally. His gritstone routes still rank with the finest and include great classics: Great Western (VS), 1946, the Girdle Traverse (HVS) and Birdlime Traverse

(HVS), 1946, all on Almscliffe, and Beeline (HVS), 1948, which he soloed, and Curving Corner (HVS), 1947, both on Ilkley.

Arthur had immediately made a great impact on the climbing scene—one had only to see this boy climbing to realize that he was something very special. A well-known Lakeland climber was so impressed by the sight of Arthur romping up the hardest gritstone routes that he wrote to Len Muscroft exclaiming that he had at last seen a climber who ALMOST equalled the famous Jim Birkett in ability. Len's response was immediate: "No one compares with Birkett," was his reply. Comparison is really meaningless, however; suffice it to say that even at this early stage Arthur Dolphin was obviously brilliant.

Even though Arthur was superbly fit and an outstanding rock athlete, he looked anything but. Peter Harding, a major pioneer on southern Gritstone and in Wales, described his first meeting with Dolphin on a winter day at Black Rocks. He had just led a party up the difficult Stonnis Crack "and was at the top when he noticed a tall and lanky figure below him. The climber was dressed in a black overcoat, maroon beret and clutching a small leather attaché case. He was blue with cold and shivering noticeably and on his feet he wore a pair of ordinary black shoes. A couple of seconds later the figure had climbed the route and stood next to Peter, hands in overcoat pockets. Peter announced himself, and the figure held out his hand and said 'Arthur Dolphin'."

As war restrictions on movement and resources gradually began to ease, Arthur again became able to visit the Lakeland Fells. Windy Ridge (S) on the sombre Ennerdale face of Gable Crag was his first Lakeland new route, put up in September 1944. As a climb it was pleasant enough but it has nothing of the power of, say, Herford's or Birkett's opening routes. Arthur was feeling his way, gaining valuable topographical knowledge, and great things were soon to follow.

Next season hosted three new Dolphin routes, and one of these, a VS named, appropriately enough, Demon Wall, indicated his true potential for technical climbing. It is a good climb without being an outstanding natural line. (A natural line is an obvious feature on a crag such as a groove, crack or ramp, e.g. the Great Flake crack of Central Buttress or the ramp of Overhanging Bastion.) This route can be regarded as contrasting his gritstone outlook on climbing, that is the capacity for climbing hard new problems on small crags that have a large number of existing routes (where it is the delight of the individual moves that counts) and the wider pioneering qualities that enabled him to discover and climb his later great Lakeland routes. It is a recognized fact that a number of climbers who reach a high technical standard on the low-altitude gritstone crags are often unable to apply themselves successfully to the much larger Lakeland precipices. This is especially true as far as new routes are concerned. Those climbers who have bridged this gap have of course been outstanding not only on British rock but much further afield also (e.g. Joe Brown and Don Whillans).

Dolphin was successful in achieving this. On Demon Wall it could be considered that the lower pitches provide merely a harder alternative to the delightful Tophet Wall (Kelly, 1923) but the top pitch moves across the great slab giving independent and difficult climbing. It is the upper section that bears the true Dolphin hallmark, and here the climbing is imaginative, technical and exposed.

Friend and fellow Leeds University student A. B. Gilchrist said of Arthur's preparation for the climb: "I was with him on Demon Wall which he gardened with a top rope before leading it. I remember sitting at the top with about 200ft. of rope paid out to Arthur below. He had been unable to make himself heard to me at the top to take the rope in because of a high wind. I was startled to see his head appear over the top—he had virtually soloed it!"

The following year produced a number of routes. On Gimmer Crag in Langdale, Whit's End (VS), climbed a steep and bold layback crack to the right of Birkett's F Route. The wall above the crack was very thin and capped by a substantial overhang. Arthur, after much trying, was forced to evade the difficulties by a rightward traverse—hence the name. Again in Langdale the two routes Proteus and Deuterus on the friendly Raven Crag, Walthwaite (a crag poised on the steep Northern Valley wall just above, and easily seen from, Chapel Stile), look innocuous enough. They are, however, both surprisingly technical climbs— on the former it is particularly desperate to leave the ground! Medusa Wall on Esk Buttress, situated high above upper Eskdale, gives a delightfully airy and much-photographed route.

But it was in 1948, with his ascent of Kipling Groove, that Arthur really shook the climbing world.

The north-west face of Gimmer Crag is one of the most spectacular and aesthetic pieces of Lakeland rock. Poised on the steep, sweeping fellside between the Langdale Pikes, Pike of Stickle and Harrison Stickle, Gimmer rests like some circular citadel on the brink of a precipice. Its cylindrical shape curves round from the east, from where it emerges, to the west, where it re-enters the hillside. This fine naked piece of rock had attracted climbers from the very earliest days, but even so in 1948 the north-west face remained inviolate.

This is not surprising for the face, nightmarishly steep, is broken in its verticality only by overhangs. From the gully floor it is some two hundred feet high, and the top hundred feet overhang the bottom, separated by a noticeable overlap. On the left lies Gimmer Crack (VS, 1928), and on the right is F Route (VS, 1941), but the main central section remained virgin. All climbers knew of its status, admired it longingly from the gully floor and patiently waited for a 'superstar' to shatter its impossibility.

In 1948 the face was examined in earnest by Jim Birkett, who abseiled down and 'gardened' the most feasible line. He knew it would go and freely passed the information on to the young Arthur Dolphin. Arthur, engrossed in the arduous task of pro-ducing the then new Langdale climbing guidebook for the F&RCC, was not prepared to let all the 'plums' fall to other climbers. He was up on Gimmer like a shot, top-roped the line three times and then climbed it.

Kipling Groove is a magnificently hard and fine route. Imme-diately difficult and exposed high on the face, it follows the overlap horizontally leftwards then breaks upwards via a steep groove. The groove ends in an overhang, and the crux of the climb lies in surmounting this to gain the vertical wall above. It is often quoted as being the first of the 'fly on the wall' climbs, and the analogy is apt, for the route can be seen to herald a new era of climbing—that of the modern Extreme.

Although not technically Extreme—the first Extreme was put up by Birkett the following year (Harlot Face-Castle Rock, 1949)—it is certainly Extreme in concept. Such was its status in the climbing world that, even when I began rock climbing in the late 1960s, Kipling Groove was THE route to do for the aspiring 'tiger'. (In the sixties the term 'tiger' was popularly addressed to climbers who sought to climb the hardest routes.) This was, in many ways, surprising, because by then another climbing era, due especially to the influence of Joe Brown, Don Whillans and Pete Crew, was well underway, with many climbs considerably harder than Kipling Groove. The fact is that Kipling Groove not only set the standard but also captured the climbing world's imagination, as had Napes Needle, Botterill's Slab, Central Buttress and Overhanging Bastion. They always will, whatever may follow.

The route and its ascent were steeped in controversy. Many thought that Birkett would be understandably peeved that this brilliant climb had been snatched from under his nose. Dolphin was also criticized when he sent a number of people signed photographs of his first ascent. In turn, when Joe Brown made a second ascent, he hammered in a piton for protection below the crux, and their outcry was against this. People claimed that Brown had despoiled the route and that this was an unjustifiable act. Arthur, in fact, led the line with only a few line slings for protection, and these were some forty feet below the crux moves, making an outstandingly bold climb.

The criticisms originated, of course, from the 'armchair pundits', those climbers who did not know the individuals involved and who had no first-hand knowledge of the climb. The emotions and feelings of those involved in the climb were quite different from those popularly imagined. That Arthur, a modest man almost to the point of shyness, should be criticized for sending photographs to people he regarded as friends was quite ridiculous: he was obviously delighted purely with the climbing of Kipling Groove. As for Joe Brown putting in a peg—well, Joe had no previous knowledge of the route and was climbing it in the rain.

If anything, Jim Birkett was nightly delighted for Arthur making the prestigious ascent, his only comment about the affair being, "There was no competition at all between Arthur and myself. We often met but never climbed together. It is true that we were both looking at the wall on Gimmer, and Arthur was the first to climb it, but it really didn't matter a jot who climbed it first. Kipling Groove is a very fine and open climb—quite tricky in clinkers!" Jim also climbed it without clipping into the peg, and this became the aim of every would-be leader. In fact, the peg has been removed and then replaced on a number of occasions since.

As for my first venture onto Kipling Groove, I was sixteen and I had very little in the way of modern equipment, although more than Arthur Dolphin some twenty years previously. For months I had been worrying about whether I could lead the route without clipping my ropes into the peg for security. It became a titanic inner battle, for clipping into the peg meant 'failure', yet if I did not do so, and I fell from the crux, then the consequences would be all too obviously dire. Rarely have I been so tense before a climb. When I reached the crux, however, I found that the decision had already been made for me—the peg had been removed. It was as if a condemned man had been reprieved at the last possible opportunity. Perhaps strangely I found the crux and the rest of the climb easy, an anticlimax, for the difficulties for me had been purely mental. Kipling Groove was a watershed, and I began leading Extreme climbs immediately afterwards.

Following Kipling Groove with new routes of equal stature and quality was a daunting task, but Dolphin more than fulfilled it with a series of fine modern routes that confirmed that a new era and a new generation of climbers had arrived. Gimmer Girdle (HVS) and Girdle Traverse (VS) on Pavey Ark were interesting excursions, but 1951 provided two remarkable routes, both climbed with A. D. Brown. Rubicon Groove (E1) on Bowfell Buttress was, as the name suggests, bold and committing; Deer Bield Buttress (E1) was a technical masterpiece, boldly climbing up the stark slaty rock of Deer Bield Crag, Easedale. The line had been tried by a number of parties, all of whom were defeated by the initial overhanging chimney. Even the meteoric R. V. M. Barry could not 'peg' (that is to climb using pitons for aid) this initial section. The 'Buttress' was another plumb line, comparable to, but harder than, the great Kipling Groove.

Arthur met and began to climb with P. J. Greenwood, who was one of 'the Bradford Lads'. Rough, tough, outrageous and extrovert, Pete was a vastly different character to the modest Dolphin. Reputedly the only person for whom Greenwood had any respect was Arthur, and this is confirmed by a number of unprintable stories of his notorious deeds.

Greenwood was, however, a very fine and ambitious climber. He provided the vital competitive spur that drove Arthur to climb great things. Together, with Pete Greenwood leading some very hard pitches, they put up some of Britain's hardest routes. In 1952 they consolidated the new Extreme grade of climbing with

Sword of Damocles on Cambridge Crag, Bowfell, and the impressively steep Hell's Groove on Scafell's East Buttress. Dolphin's last Lakeland new route was Communist Convert (VS), 1953, on the very steep and hitherto unclimbed Raven Crag, Thirlmere. It is good, hard for its grade and considered the classic route of this very hard crag.

An interesting feature of these later great routes was that they quickly received second ascents and soon became popular. There was no aura of impossibility enveloping these climbs as there was surrounding the early 'Rock and Ice' routes. (The Rock and Ice were a group of hard climbers headed by Joe Brown and Don Whillans who built up a tremendous reputation for putting up very hard rock climbs, particularly noted for the development of the great Clogwyn d'ur Arddu—Wales's finest cliff.) The reason for this was, not as popularly supposed, that the Rock and Ice routes were harder, but that Arthur was completely free with his new route information. He would give anyone who was genuinely interested accurate and unexaggerated facts about his climbs, the holds, the moves, the dangers and the difficulties. There was no 'bull', just a genuine desire that others should do his routes and enjoy them. Contrast with this, say, Dovedale Grooves (E1, Brown/Whillans, 1953), which did not receive a second ascent for ten years, chiefly because the majority of climbers had no information as to its location or difficulty.

"Ginger" Cain, an acquaintance and occasional climbing partner of Arthur's, said:

> He had begun to open up routes of a new standard in the Lakes comparable to those of the Rock and Ice in Wales. He created some classic routes that were often repeated soon afterwards, but this I think was due largely to his open and guileless personality. He would give detailed descriptions and advice on climbs to anyone who asked.
>
> I also believe that had he lived the Rock and Ice myth would not have developed—he would have repeated their routes and would have told anyone who asked what they were really like.

Arthur's greatest ambitions, however, lay in the Alps and beyond; to climb big mountains was his ultimate goal. Although by 1953 he had five Alpine seasons to his credit, with some good routes accomplished (including the Traverse of the Drus, the Zmutt Ridge of the Matterhorn, the North Ridge of the Aiguille

Peigne and the Moming of the Einal Rotthorn), he obtained a reputation of suffering from altitude sickness. Certainly Arthur's Alpine record did not match his rock-climbing achievements, but it is only partly true that he had a 'height ceiling'. True he suffered terribly in the high Alps, but really this was due to the way he had so far tackled Alpine climbing. With only a few precious weeks to spare for holidays a year (Arthur was a conscientious and important metallurgist), he treated the high mountains like his local gritstone outcrops. He threw himself at them, tornado-like, but acutely lacked experience or even preparedness.

Jack Bloor recalls one of his early Alpine sorties:

In the early days Arthur was not a good Alpinist. We set off from Montenveres to climb the Mère de Glace face of the Grepon and failed to reach the Tour Rouge hut (and Point Albert) and were forced to sit out in gaberdine anoraks just below the hut because we failed to locate it in the darkness—we discovered our battery lamps were knackered. The next day we rested eating only a few boiled sweets Arthur had remembered to stuff in his pockets. We then climbed the Mère de Glace face of the Grepon but were very slow—Arthur insisted on free climbing the hardest cracks he could find! We had a tricky descent down the Nantillon Glacier in the dark, to arrive at the Montenveres at the same time as the experienced parties were preparing to leave! (An Alpine start is generally around 4 o'clock in the morning!)

Arthur had in fact been considered for the 1953 (successful) Everest Expedition but was passed by because of his 'altitude ceiling'. But if the summer expedition failed, then it was to be tackled again later in the season, and he was to be reconsidered. In Arthur's mind his selection depended on a good 1953 Alpine performance. This he was determined to achieve, and he accepted a new post at Calder Hall on the West Cumbrian coast, which left him with the summer free to spend in the Alps. The world seemingly lay at his feet, for with the time to acclimatize he knew he could master his mountain sickness, and his technical ability was never in doubt.

It was not to be, for after making the first British ascent of an ED route, the south face of the Dent du Géant, with a Belgian climber, André Colard, he was tragically killed on an easy descent. Characteristically he had descended to the foot of the face to pick up both rucksacks and was walking down the descent path. Rounding a rocky protuberance, possibly the combined weight of the rucksacks forced him off balance. He slipped onto an easy snow slope, slid and hit his head. Death was instantaneous.

Only a handful of climbers were there to attend the funeral at Courmayeur. Tough men, seasoned Alpinists and hard rock climbers paid tribute with tears openly flowing down their cheeks. His fiancée arrived in Chamonix a few days later, having intended to stay and climb with him, for they had frequently climbed together in the Lakes; on their return they were to have been married.

> Into my heart an air that kills
> From yon far country blows:
> What are those blue remembered hills,
> What spires, what farms are those?

A man for all seasons, Arthur had been hero and friend to both the 'old guard' climbing establishment and the new wave of climbers. Perhaps uniquely, he was respected and liked by all. He was intelligent and sincere, yet his personality seemed almost contradictory in its diversity. A man of great personal courage, yet modest to the point of shyness, athletic, with tremendous finger strength, he always appeared anaemic, friendly and helpful and yet ultra-competitive; apparently reserved he yet had a fine, wry 'English' sense of humour. Harold Drasdo, an accomplished climber and acquaintance wrote: "His reputation in the climbing world combined with his gentleness of manner made him one apart from all of us. He was a legend to all but his most intimate friends. I'm not sure that even they could have known him deeply—sometimes you sensed a sort of loneliness in him."

Despite his "gentleness of manner", Arthur was prepared to push himself to the limits of his physical and mental capacity. He once set out to run the Yorkshire Three Peaks (a famous twenty-four-mile fell race), with Jack Bloor and Des Birch. Pushing himself hard to keep up with the better-practised runners, he literally passed out on his feet. On completion of the course he had to be revived in a bath of cold water. In the Alps, when he and MacNaught Davis took a routine stop for a rest, Arthur removed his boots to reveal socks soaked in blood! He had not slackened his pace or mentioned the predicament previously.

His modesty was well illustrated one day when he was sitting in the Old Dungeon Ghyll bar with his fiancée, Marie Ball. It was Marie's birthday and they had just made the first ascent of Babylon on Far East Raven Crag, a climb which is now graded Extremely Severe (E1 5b). A likely looking youth started talking with them and as he supped his pint he explained that he was a budding 'tiger'. In fact that day he had been climbing with the great Arthur Dolphin! What routes they had done! The unlikely looking Arthur drank his orange juice, quietly smiled, said nothing and left. His departure left the bar echoing laughter as the youth was informed as to just whom he had been talking to.

Occasionally though, Arthur would react to other people's imposed opinions. One very wet day, at a Leeds University meet during the war, somebody soloed up Innominate Crack (VS) on Great Gable wearing the new 'tricounis' (nailed boots with large teeth like nails around the toe). Most people were sheltering and waiting for the rain to stop. Arthur attempted the climb in his old 'clinker' nailed boots, to everyone's amusement, on slimy rock, and he failed to do it despite a number of attempts. His old boots just shot off the smooth and very greasy rock. Retreating, he was greeted by laughter from the watching climbers. Amid further laughter he grabbed the successful climber, stripped off the fellow's boots, donned them and flew up the climb.

Arthur was inwardly determined that he should not be bettered in anything he did. He was truly competitive and set himself standards he thought imperative to fulfil. Almscliffe was of course Dolphin's crag, and his exploits there, above all others, epitomized the competitive ethic.

Not only did he solo the hardest climbs there but he continually strove to reduce the time of his ascents—twenty seconds per route was typical. Crampons were worn, and he still climbed the routes with apparent ease! Birdlime Traverse (HVS) Almscliffe's hardest route at that time, was climbed for the first time by Dolphin in midweek, when he heard that southern gritstone expert Peter Harding was coming to attempt the line the next weekend. Because of Dolphin's commitment to his work, he never climbed on midweek days, other than holidays. Harding had to settle for a second ascent, that of the bold and committing Great Western, and he wrote: "When I did the second independent ascent of his (Dolphin's) Great Western, he soloed up in boots (clinkers) afterwards, taking the Direct Finish. He had a spectacular way of doing Great Western by swinging his arms like a trapeze artist. He enjoyed being spectacular and was great to watch."

Of course Arthur was such a prolific climber that he had his failures, and those include an early attempt on Cenotaph Corner where he actually free-climbed past Joe Brown's initial aid points but then retreated. He made no excuses and remarked accurately: "I wasn't good enough on the day." This simple, truthful comment has subsequently provided solace and hope for many climbers and has become a famous piece of climbing rhetoric.

Attempting Central Buttress on Scafell in nailed boots, he fell from the flake crack much to the amazement of the watching climbers gathered below. He had tried to lay back up the impending flake with total disregard of his footwear. Consequently his nailed boots had skidded off the wall where rubbers would have stayed put.

But Dolphin did so much that there were bound to be failures, and they did nothing to tarnish his reputation. His climbing performances other than those of pioneering new routes were remarkable. Chuck Hudson wrote in a letter to Bill Peascod: "What d'you think of Dolphin's effort on Mon, Deer Bield Crack (walked from Dungeon Ghyll), Botterills Slab (Scafell) Sepulchre and down Kern Knotts Crack (Gable) and walked back to Dungeon Ghyll, first two climbs being wet; result one easy day."

Arthur possessed a keen brain and a dry sense of humour. Once challenged to memorize the first forty verses of Kubla Khan in an evening, by Jack Bloor, he did so without a single mistake, and it provided him with a route name as well:

> In Xanadu did Kubla Khan,
> A stately pleasure dome decree,
> Where Alph the sacred river ran,
> Through caverns measureless to man,
> Down to a sunless sea. . . .

Alph (VS) on Pavey Ark was the name used, and it fits the rather damp and meandering route very well. Many of his route names also illustrate his humour: Kipling Groove (HVS), so named because it was "Ruddy Hard"; Communist Convert (VS), named because it goes from left to right; Samaritan Corner (HS), so named because it was often passed by. An article entitled 'What's in a name', written by Dolphin, told the stories behind his route names. He finished the article thus: "The holiday reached its climax with the ascent of Kipling Groove, and so on the final day we were even content to sun bathe in the perfect weather. We couldn't have climbed anyway—we had exhausted our stock of names."

Arthur was slow to accept new equipment but when he saw its worth, he employed it. He had nylon ropes and thin nylon slings which could be threaded more easily around chockstones or placed on much smaller flakes than the thick and cumbersome hemp ropes used by his predecessors. He frowned on the general use of pitons but, after his Alpine experiences, designed and made some very thin ones out of hardened steel. These were intended for use in hair-line cracks and were similar to the modern RURP (Realized Ultimate Reality Piton) produced in America.

His climbing footwear was the Dunlop Green Flash, a shoe designed for running—indeed, he would do both in the same pair. Despite some improvements in Dolphin's equipment, he never realized the true potential of jamming chockstones in cracks for protection or using other forms of running belays. Others had already begun to exploit these techniques to some effect, e.g. Joe Brown and Don Whillans. In part he owed his allegiance to another generation and never really accepted these practices as quite the thing to do.

Arthur was the inspiration to a new generation of climbers, for the Extreme men of the 1950s and sixties were a breed different from that of Birkett and Peascod. Yet he seemed suspended between the two generations, a delicate bridge spanning the transition between the great unprotected leads and the use of more sophisticated protection and equipment. He earned the respect and friendship of his contemporaries and has become a legend to the present climbing generation. Although it is hard to believe, Arthur Dolphin was just twenty-eight years old when he died.

Route name	Grade	Location	Comments
1944 Windy Ridge	S	Gable Crag	
1945 Demon Wall	VS	Tophet Wall, Great Gable	
Tophet Girdle	HS	Tophet Wall, Great Gable	
Nocturne	MVS	Gimmer Crag, Langdale	
1946 Monkey Puzzle	HS	Deer Bield, Easdale	
1947 Limpet Grooves	MVS	Side Pike, Langdale	
Garden Path	VD	White Ghyll	
Whits End	VS	Gimmer Crag	
Protus	VS	Raven Crag, Walthwaite	
Deuterus	VS	Raven Crag, Walthwaite	
Hobsons Choice	HS	Pavey Ark	
Medusa Wall	VS	Esk Buttress, Scafell	
Gargoyle Grooves	VS	Esk Buttress, Scafell	
1948 Samaritan Corner	HS	Gimmer Crag	
Alph	MVS	Pavey Ark	
Kipling Groove	HVS	Gimmer Crag	
1949 Watson Wall	HS	East Raven Crag, Langdale	
Baskerville	MVS	East Raven Crag, Langdale	
Stewpot	HS	East Raven Crag, Langdale	
Gimmer Girdle	HVS	Gimmer Crag	
Russett Groove	VD	White Ghyll	
Inferno	HS	White Ghyll	
1950 Girdle Traverse	VS	Pavey Ark	
1951 Rubicon Groove	HVS	Bowfell	
Deer Bield Buttress	E1	Deer Bield	
Ferrous Buttress	HVS	Iron Crag, Thirlmere	
1952 Chequer Buttress	HVS	Pavey Ark	
Shivering Timber	VS	White Ghyll	
Sword of Damocles	E1	Bowfell	Alt. with P. J. Greenwood
Dunmail Cracks	HVS	Deer Bield	
1952 Pegasus	HVS	East Buttress, Scafell	Alt. with P. J. Greenwood
Hell's Groove	E1	East Buttress, Scafell	P. J. Greenwood led overhanging crack
Trespasser's Groove	HVS	Esk Buttress	
Babylon	E1	Far East Raven Crag, Langdale	With Marie Ball

Route name	Grade	Location	Comments
1953 Communist Convert	VS	Raven Crag, Thirlmere	First route on an important crag

11
John Alan Austin
(1934–   )

When in 1954 a twenty-year-old Yorkshire youth was demobbed after two years' National Service, the wind of change was blowing through the climbing world. The sport had now been opened to all social classes; both transport and the means to pay for 'weekends away' were available to the majority. Although the youth knew nothing of it, the direction of free rock climbing hung precariously in the balance.

Up to now, climbing using rock pitons (a piton is made of hardened steel and driven into a crack in the rock in much the same way as a nail is driven into a piece of wood) for direct climbing aid or even for protection (placed to act as a running belay only) had been shunned by the pioneers. Their use was considered almost sinful on British rock. The big and hard Lakeland routes pioneered by Birkett, Peascod and Dolphin did not employ pitons, their view being that to use a piton was to defeat the whole object of technical rock climbing. To do so was to 'murder the impossible' and remove the great physical and psychological barriers.

The use of the piton had become extensive on the Continent, especially in the Alps and the Dolomites. Here on the big rock and mixed mountain faces (that is, faces consisting of rock, snow and ice climbing—such as the north face of the Eiger) there seemed ample justification. Advances in metal technology and production techniques were making the piton into a very sophisticated and readily available weapon.

Many climbers in Britain began to accept and use the piton. Unfortunately, a not inconsiderable number of climbers used the piton totally unscientifically and quite indiscriminately. Not only were pitons regularly used on new ascents but certain unscrupulous climbers placed them on routes that had been done without. Suddenly ordinary mortals could 'climb' the coveted Very Severe grade. A fashion sprang up to hang round the bars in Langdale and Borrowdale with a 'peg hammer' stuck brazenly on one's belt. It seemed that the majority wanted the soft option.

The Yorkshire youth became a climber simply because his mother decided he should have a hobby to keep him occupied in the evening and accordingly enrolled him for night school. The course happened to be rock climbing, and the youth was Alan Austin. During the next twenty years Alan climbed and pioneered an almost uncountable number of routes. Most significantly, however, he stood and openly fought against the use of the piton. Thankfully he tipped the scales in the favour of free rock climbing.

Born in Bradford, where he still lives and runs a climbing shop, in 1934 he was educated at Thornton Grammar School. Leaving at the age of sixteen, he joined the family wool business. It was on the climbing course that he met Brian Evans. Brian was young and keen, a committed climber who persuaded Alan, because he had a van, to climb in the Lakes. Reluctant at first, Alan eventually agreed upon the journey when it was explained that the petrol cost could be split four ways.

They soon started knocking off the classic VS climbs and began ticking off Dolphin's great routes. Often working on Saturday mornings, they would climb on gritstone in the afternoon and drive to the Lakes on the Sunday morning. It was not long before Austin was climbing two or three nights a week in his local gritstone outcrops. Winter weekends were spent in Derbyshire and it was there, whatever the weather, where Alan served his climbing apprenticeship. In the early 1950s he met the most famous climber of them all, Joe Brown, on Curbar Edge. The meeting had a profound influence on him for he was awakened to modern concepts in protection and, of course, technique.

Austin was attempting a crack in the Dead Bay area of Curbar Edge. He had been on the problem for some hours and was on the verge of giving up when "two short men with long arms" arrived on the scene. One of these characters was Joe Brown, and naturally his presence on the scene intimated to Austin that he must climb the crack. It was unthinkable that a Yorkshireman could be seen to fail in the presence of one from Lancashire! He again flung himself at the crack but to little avail, and he quickly found himself deposited at the bottom again.

"Eeeh lad," said Joe, "why not try this in there?" On speaking he picked up a gritstone flag, broke it to size in his bare hands and advised Alan to use it as a chockstone runner, at this point in the crack where Alan had been failing. "I'll put it in fer yer." Joe soled up the crack and dropped it in at the required height. It fitted perfectly.

Inspired by the new-found runner (i.e. a sling which would be threaded round the chockstone and utilized as a running relay), Alan forced himself up the crack. As he reached the overhangs which lay at the top of the crack, he found himself physically and mentally drained, and his runner now hung way below him. He began to shake so violently that not only was he convinced he would fall but the people on the ground thought so too. Joe was so convinced that he ran to the top of the crag to give Alan a hand up. This in itself must have been a unique occasion, as the 'master' is by no means noted for his benevolence to mere mortals. Anyway, pulling out all the stops, Alan scraped his way up the final few feet and completed a very hard climb.

When Alan arrived back at the foot of the crack, Joe exclaimed: "By gum lad, that looks hard." He promptly soloed it in faultless style.

Alan said: "I learnt a lot from this incident, and within a year I think the gap in both technique and use of protection had narrowed considerably."

Brown's concepts in protection were certainly advanced, and these innovations in thinking about protection placement, coupled, of course, with great natural ability and dedication, were responsible for pushing up standards throughout Britain. Brown, however, unlike Austin, did not significantly affect the Lakeland scene, for his Lakeland new routes can be counted on the fingers of one hand almost. Admittedly they are, without exception, brilliant and hard routes, but he never really consolidated his position as he did in Wales and elsewhere.

The climbing lesson administered by Brown was not only significant for Alan but timely also. Up to this point his ambitions and eagerness to climb were undoubtedly outstripping his ability and rational judgement. On Almscliffe he had narrowly escaped death when he fell from what was to become a hard Austin climb, Western Front (XS); he hit the ground miraculously, landing relatively unhurt among the boulders below. On Malham Cove, the natural limestone amphitheatre that is the pride of the Yorkshire Dales National Park, he was not so lucky. Climbing with his wife-to-be, he was some thirty feet above the very steep hillside when he pulled hard on a limestone block. The block parted company with the cliff, and Alan fell hard to the ground below. This time he spent the rest of the summer recovering from his injuries.

Emerging from these early epics and his Derbyshire and Yorkshire gritstone experience came a flood of new routes. He was especially active in the Lake District and on both Yorkshire gritstone and limestone. It should not be forgotten, however, that he has pioneered rock climbs throughout Britain.

Of these his Hanging Slab on Sgurr Mhic Coinnich (Black Cuillins—Skye) takes the most obvious line to the right of King Cobra (Bonnington and Patey). When Alan made the first ascent, he led out over two hundred feet of rope in most impressive surroundings. With Evans and Fuller he put up Nightshade on the great granite cliffs of the Poisoned Glen. This is Alan's favourite new route, and quite simply the few who have had the privilege to climb there reckon it to be the finest route in Ireland. It is an eight-hundred-foot line up a massive and otherwise virgin granite cliff. It was climbed because Austin, due for his annual two-week holiday and bound for Chamonix, did something out of the ordinary. On hearing the usually bad weather reports from the Alps, he changed plans and decided to investigate Ireland. Instead of the usual depressing days in the Flesh Pits of

Chamonix waiting for the illusive good weather, it was Guinness and Nightshade in Ireland—who could ask for more?

Significantly, but going almost unnoticed, he free-climbed the lassoe pitch on White Slab E1-5C Clogwyn d'ur Arddu (Wales) by boldly moving up the very thin arete and then traversing across the slab above the aid spike (1959). Outside the Lakes his most famous routes, however, lie on the Yorkshire gritstone. He notably increased the standard with a succession of routes: High Street, Ilkley (1956), The Shelf, Crookside (1957), Western Front, Almscliffe (1958), and Wall of Horrors, Almscliffe (1961), a successful lead of Arthur Dolphin's famous problem (Dolphin top-roped the route but never managed to lead it).

It is with the Lake District, however, that Austin's name has been inextricably linked, particularly in his dogmatic views on free climbing and his close association with the Langdale Valley. His routes span a period of twenty-one years from 1956 (Stickle Grooves HVS on Pavey Ark) to 1975 (Overhang Pitch HVS on Dow Crag). He climbed some seventy-five new routes, and more than half of these are in the Langdale area.

Development of the big and rambling Pavey Ark was, perhaps, his most significant contribution. At first acquaintance it is hard to be inspired by Pavey, for it looks scrappy and vegetated: it in no way compares with the great cliffs of Scafell or the Eastern Fells (Dove Crag and Castle Rock). Investigate further, however, and there is much rock to be found hidden among the vastness; indeed the East Wall is most impressive.

Stickle Grooves was climbed one day when Austin was aiming to do Dolphin's Chequers, Buttress, (HVS). He noticed the wall of unclimbed rock and ventured up the obvious, and somewhat insecure, groove. This was typical Austin, for his approach to new routes seemed, at first, quite random. The results were variable and occasionally magnificent.

Outstanding, by any standard, was his ascent of Astra E2 5b. Alternating leads with 'Matie' Metcalf produced a beautiful, very bold and technically difficult route up the two-hundred-foot blank-looking pillar that stands out on the East Wall of Pavey Ark. To the climber Astra has that rare magic which is some function of rock quality, line, boldness and difficulty. Indeed, many consider it to be one of the finest climbs in Langdale.

These days it is surrounded by a complicated web of new and

much harder routes. They are excellent climbs, but nevertheless they seem overshadowed by the greatness of Astra. The route is probably the best introduction to modern Extreme climbing. A bold and fingery start allows one to gain a rib of rock in the middle of space; a small runner placed awkwardly allows some relaxation, moves left and up an ever-steeping wall end after a further forty feet. From here a blind move rightwards across the verticality enables the hands to be placed, at full stretch, on the sloping edge of a rock ledge hidden somewhere above your head. A very committing and strenuous pull lands you above the difficulties and to a belay that is exactly right. Below lie vertical and over-hanging rock and exposure heightened by the east gully falling rapidly away to Stickle Tarn; above there is a further 150 feet of steep rocks which culminates in a difficult and often wet chimney.

'Matie' led through and the climb was completed. Position is superb; rock is beautifully hard, clean and bubbly; line is impec-cable and uncomplicated. I once asked Alan which were his favourite new routes: mentioning Pavey Ark, he talked a little about 'the Bracken Clock' (E2 5C 5B, 1970), the crux slab being the most gritstone-like piece of rock in the Lakes; then in a short terse sentence he said, "Astra, we were busting with pride when we did that." No further comment was needed.

The ascent of Astra, in 1961, is also an example of theoretical and practical ethics. Austin was, of course, the man who stood out against pegs and voiced bitter objection against those who used them, whilst Eric ('Matie') Metcalf could himself be called the ultimate purist. Yet on Astra Austin put in a peg, and used it, as in fact he did on a number of ascents including Rainmaker (HVS), Man of Straw (E1), Arcturus (HVS), Red Groove (HVS) and Brackenclock (E2). Yet today, without exception, all these routes are climbed free. The cynic may describe this as hypocritical but it must be looked at in the context of the era. At this time, particularly based in Borrowdale, a large number of climbers, including a number of competent pioneers, were using pitons without a thought of free climbing. Austin was against this, and if he failed in his rigid ideals—well, he is only human, but more importantly he succeeded in directing the course of rock climbing towards free climbing, and this was a truly remarkable achieve-ment.

Further to this, I do not know anybody, today, who would

criticize him for popping that peg in Astra. It remains *in situ* and is used even now, as a runner. When Austin climbed these routes, they could not be protected with nut runners to the same extent as they are today.

An example of 'Matie' Metcalf's purity of ethics was witnessed when one day on the East Buttress of Scafell he dropped a sling, attempting to thread a runner while leading, and refused to have it returned to him, although it would have been a comparatively easy task to do so. His line of reasoning was that it could not have been done on a large Alpine face and that it was bad form. Conceding it to be an unforgivable mistake, he proceeded to lead the pitch without the protection.

Actually, 'Matie' was a brilliant climber, and a hard man. He did a number of difficult first ascents, usually with Austin, and a number of unrecorded second ascents of Rock and Ice routes in Wales. I once had the privilege to climb with 'Matie'. It was a very wet day in Borrowdale, and I tried to interest him in what was then a peg route. Well, he seemed interested and we roped up. It was only when I actually started climbing that I realized that the only way I was going to be allowed to climb it was free—he would not let me use the pegs as runners. I did not argue—just climbed.

During this period and up to the mid 1960s, Langdale and Borrowdale became the main Lakeland climbing centres. Possibly the demise of Wasdale Head as the focus of Lakeland climbing started when Jim Birkett put up his superb routes right across the Lake District. It was completed when transport, mainly in the form of the motorbike, allowed a different social class to go where it pleased. The scene became rough, tough, pretentious and rowdy. In Langdale it was based around the Wall End Barn where the would-be climbers congregated and slept. The barn, situated next to the road, became grossly abused, and the police intervened, but the crowd simply moved to Stool End Barn instead. It became a whole way of life to many. It is easy to see its attraction, in the context of the era. Wild motorcycle rides ending in uninhibited freedom from organization and discipline must have been very attractive to the working populace of the time. It was pure escapism and, compared with the clinically organized and regimented camp sites of today, for some it still has a certain appeal.

In this scene heroes were left unchallenged, and to a certain extent climbing development stagnated. Alan Austin wrote:

The early fifties was also a time then East Raven enjoyed its burst of popularity. These little crags, stretching down from Raven Crag itself towards the New Dungeon Ghyll Hotel, had been by-passed by climbers of earlier generations. But now they became covered in a network of short routes reminiscent of gritstone climbs. It is probably not true to say that the climbers concerned were alcoholics, but it is certain that the Old Hotel and its nearness to the crags was an important factor in explorations carried out at that time—and indeed, in climbing there today.

Of course, there are many tales of the deeds and notorious doings of his era. One of my favourites is of one night in the Stool End Barn. Don Whillans (a hard, uncompromising man and one of the best rock climbers and mountaineers Britain has produced), the ultimate toughie, was struggling to get to sleep among the usual rowdy behaviour that went on after the pub. His voice grunted out, "Shut up." The response from the barn was of course predictable: "Who says?" Don replied: "Whillans." Dead silence followed.

The scene in Borrowdale was similar, with climbers and hangers-on all occupying the boulders beneath Falcon Crags or the caves of the Bowderstone Quarry. This quarry has now collapsed, as has the whole social scene. The wind of change significantly altered course.

Two different 'camps' arose, and attitudes in each were quite different. They were surprisingly insular and like trogs did not often leave their respective valleys. When the two 'camps' met on a neutral crag, such as Castle Rock, the barracking was intense but good-humoured, Ian ('Sherpa') Roper recalls: "One day on Castle Rock I was attempting 'Last Laugh'. 'Rossey' and his mates arrived on the crag and proceeded to 'rag' me. In the end I so lost confidence I was forced to retreat. The Borrowdale team had won the day."

Borrowdale climbers, however, became far too fond of the piton, probably the leading light being P. Ross, but there were a number of good climbers and many not so good, with attitudes quite different to the Langdale clientele. They became known, ungloriously, as 'the iron men'. In Langdale the influence of Birkett and Dolphin, particularly the incident where Joe Brown was heavily censured for making an early ascent of Kipling

Groove with a peg, combined with the propaganda of Sid Cross (by then the landlord at the Old Dungeon Ghyll Hotel) and the rigid ethics and caustic tongue of Alan Austin, the leading activist, kept aided climbing to a minimum.

By 1966 it was time for a new Langdale guidebook for the 1950s guidebook written by Dolphin (Cook) was by now hopelessly out of date. Alan Austin seemed the natural successor to Dolphin and, conveniently, within a short space of time he joined the FRCC and was then asked to do the guide. (The FRCC of course publish the *Lake District Definitive Rock Climbing Guides*.) The produced work was excellent, for it had significantly advanced from the earlier guides and fully coped with the volume of new routes and their increased difficulty. It took a firm, but just, ethical line and also had a (long overdue) revised system of grading. The format was different, and it sported a robust plastic cover. The latter may seem a trivial point, but it is symbolic of the new thinking behind the guide. To achieve such a guide Austin had to change FRCC guidebook policy, and this brought him into a conflict with H. M. Kelly, who had been the instigator of the modern guide. Kelly was, of course, the iron hand in the iron glove but his policies were, naturally enough, somewhat outdated. After all, his first guidebooks had been produced some forty years earlier. It is rumoured that so venomous was the feeling against change that, as Austin walked into the Guidebook Committee Meeting of the FRCC, his new text was thrown with such a force that it speeded past him through the open door.

Austin, the archetypal Yorkshireman, remained singularly unmoved and went on to win the conflict. Terrier-like, so determined was he to change the system that he was quite prepared to produce the guidebook himself. This I am sure he would have done at great personal profit. After all, he had written it and he undoubtedly had the financial means to publish.

His change in the grading system was to extend the VS grade to Hard Very Severe and Extremely Severe. (Remember Jones had an Exceptionally Severe grade in the 1890s in *Climbing in the English Lake District*). Austin also extended the easier grades i.e. Severe was split into three and became Mild Severe, Severe and Hard Severe. The grouping of routes, of wide-ranging difficulty, in the Very Severe grade had become quite unacceptable. Routes such as F Route, Kipling Groove and Astra, all VS under the old system, now became respectively VS, HVS and Extremely Severe. In fact, Dolphin had formulated a new system to extend the VS grade in his guide, but unfortunately for the active climbers, he was overruled by those who no longer climbed at this standard and did not truly understand the need. The guidebook was the worse for it.

Austin was certainly not lacking in conviction but some of his ideas I do not accept. He wanted to eliminate the record of new climbs, i.e. the list of first ascents which contain in chronological order the names of the pioneers and the date the route was first climbed. His 'rationale' behind this radical concept was that he thought there would be no point in using aid or other dastardly tactics to pioneer a route if there were no egotistical reward, i.e. your name in print, having done a first ascent. Personally I find this a totally selfish attitude. The history of climbing and climbers has, obviously, fascinated me even before I started climbing. If Alan Austin had had his way on this point, there would be no record, certainly, of modern-day pioneers and their deeds. Fortunately Alan was defeated.

Those who do not think climbing a competitive sport are whimsically mistaken for it is extremely competitive at its highest level. The beauty perhaps in climbing is that the competition lies within oneself. Climbing is such a diverse activity that one can derive pleasure from it in many ways: for some an easy climb and the beauty of the mountains are enough; for others extreme technical climbing is the incentive, and of course some climbers delight in both. As in no other sport the individual defines his own parameters, and only the individual knows if he has given his best.

Alan Austin was an extremely intense climber and took it very seriously. There are stories of him, when sleeping in climbing huts, actually kicking the base of his bunk, muttering about falling and climbing during his sleep. He was a competitive climber and also deliberately secretive about his new routing activities. He did not want any other climber 'nipping in' and doing his lines.

When Austin was in his prime, the main competition for Lakeland-based climbers came from the Welsh 'raiders', Joe Brown, Don Whillans and especially the very 'pushy' Pete Crew. Quite correctly reputations and heroes meant nothing to those men, and they were involved in a headlong push, producing progressively harder routes.

One crag, Dove Crag in the eastern fells, epitomized their efforts. Each made an impressive mark on this, perhaps Lakelands most fierce crag. Joe Brown with Whillans produced Dovedale Grooves E1 (1953) a very steep and strenuous crack which lay unrepeated until Austin climbed it with Jack Soper some ten years later. Whillans returned to put up Extol E2 5C (1960), one of the Lake District's most important climbs and really a breakthrough in attitude. It takes the central most obvious line, bursting through some frightening overhangs near the top. The main pitch is intimidating and requires a full 150 feet of rope. On the first ascent Whillans and Colin Mortlock were climbing together. Bonnington described the route as "hard and uncompromising, like Whillans".

Pete Crew came along and put up the technical Hiraeth E2 (1962) but he failed, after considerable effort (and a number of attempts), to climb the overhanging North Buttress. The big overhanging wall became known as Crew's Folly due to the number of pitons and expansion bolts he used. (It was not climbed, without aid, until 1980, almost twenty years after Crew's attempts—Birkett/Graham). The 'Welshmen', then, certainly left their mark.

This competitive situation came to a head on 17th June 1962. Jack Soper had learnt of a potential route on the great Esk Buttress which lies on the Scafell Range and at the head of the Eskdale Valley. It was a much-tried line. Jim Birkett had been there in the 1940s: his Great Central Climb (VS), 1945, was an attempt which failed when the second man decided he had had enough and forced an abseil, so avoiding the main wall at the top of the Crag. Arthur Dolphin too, when climbing Trespasser Grooves (HVS), in 1952, had been forced off rightwards avoiding the main difficulties which lay up the final wall. Soper had found himself a plumb line.

He proceeded to abseil down the problematical top wall and trundled off a number of loose blocks. The stage was set for Soper, Austin and Metcalf to climb the route of the decade.

During the intervening week Soper chatted about the route, and the information was picked up by some of Pete Crew's pals. When the home team arrived at the starting-point early on the Sunday morning, they discovered to their consternation another car already there. They pounded across the Great Moss, not daring to think of the implications. On arrival at the Crag, however, their worst innermost fears were realized—Pete Crew was already on the route after making a dawn start. The Central Pillar E2, as it became known, had been snatched from underneath their noses, and worse, it had been done by a 'Welsh Raider'. Even so, Austin produced another two new routes that day. One of them he called, significantly, 'Black Sunday'.

In 1973 Austin, assisted by Rod Valentine, again updated the Langdale guide. The result was highly controversial, for many fine climbs were missed out. In my opinion a definitive guide must accurately record the climbs that are done; to miss routes out should not be the prerogative of the guide writer. The stage was set for the famous Matheson/Austin clash. Rob Matheson wrote:

> After studying Austin's and Valentine's new guide, I feel that I ought to bring certain points into the open before too many people are deceived into buying it for the wrong reasons. It is apparent that two processes have occurred; firstly the demolition of new routes to form variations on existing routes; and, secondly, the omission of harder new routes, which the writers either hadn't done or couldn't do, or which they considered used too much aid. . . .
>
> 'Cruel Sister', on the other hand, had been dismissed as an "attempt", and omitted from the guide. The "attempt" made use of a sky hook and a sling on a peg for aid, to allow a route up one of the most impressive pieces of rock on the cliff. . . .
>
> Austin also states that "one must learn to fail on a line". Well, I can now say that Austin had previously failed on this line (despite the use of tension techniques and pitons), and he appears to be condemning my efforts because he himself failed in the past. . . .
>
> In his preamble the General Editor applauds Austin and Valentine, not only for bringing the guide right up to date, but also for their determination to preserve the true spirit of rock climbing. To that, I would say the Editor 'doesn't know the half of it'.

Alan Austin replied:

> "Cruel Sister" was omitted from the guide because I did not believe it had been climbed. I cannot see how a party can claim to have been successful when, having failed on the Crux, they have simply gone round to the top of the cliff, hung a sling down over it, then swarmed up from below. Surely, rock climbing is a challenge, and superb lines like this rib throw down their challenge to succeeding generations of

climbers, until eventually along comes someone who can do the climb. I do not see crags as an impressive back-cloth where ruthless men can construct their climbs. . . .

Incidentally, I would point out that the locals do not regard me as a particularly 'pure' climber. The modern viewpoint is illustrated by a remark that floated in from the background when I was holding a runner in order to clip into it: "If it's not aid, what are you holding it for?"

With regard to my statements on Cruel Sister . . . in fact, the first ascent of Arcturus was an attempt on the rib. . . .

Again I failed. No pitons were used.

The rights and wrongs do not lay firmly one hundred per cent in either camp, and the result was good for climbing. The next generation of climbers benefited by listening and realizing that aid climbing should be avoided where possible, and the result was the birth of the 'Jackal'—a climber who went about doing free ascents of aided routes (i.e. ascents that did not employ the aid).

Climbing standards rose tremendously, and aid was used only after much heart-searching. Over the next seven years or so (up to the 1980s) brilliant, extremely difficult and beautiful climbs were done. If routes used minimal aid, then it became a great challenge to do them totally free. It was a remarkably healthy situation. The 'true' Golden Age of rock climbing had arrived.

Suppressing information, i.e. missing routes out of the guide-book, did nothing to help this situation, although I can sympathize with Austin in that certain people were not entirely truthful in recording the mode of their ascent so that, determining the truth, he became embittered against them, which considerably in-fluenced his decision. There is a distinct difference between placing an odd peg or sling for aid and declaring this and abseiling down a proposed new climb (descending on a rope) and placing all the runners and aid points prior to climbing a route. This was a purely egotistical thing to do especially as the first ascensionists concerned declared only the odd point of aid, conveniently for-getting that they had completely runnered the route prior to their ascent. Even so, all routes should have been included with the appropriate comment as to the mode of their ascent. This, in my opinion, which is of course purely theoretical and made with hindsight, would have been far more influential.

Referring to the Matheson/Austin controversy, however, as I

have said, there were rights and wrongs on both sides. Rob had put up some superb lines—his Cruel Sister on Pavey Ark is one of the great modern Lakeland routes. His style of ascent was, however, not as it should have been, so Austin was right to criticize, but I think he went too far. Had he recorded the route and the mode of ascent and expressed his dislike fairly, I think it would have influenced climbing sooner. Rob was, after all, climbing much harder routes than had previously been attempted. He was right at the forefront of development. Cruel Sister, like all the controversial routes, is now climbed totally free, so no more need really be said.

I myself suffered from Austin's rigid policies. In the very early 1970s there was a good deal of talk about new routes on a 'new crag' in Langdale—Spout Crag. On investigating, to my surprise, all the climbs lay on rather scrappy and vegetated crag well to the right of the main crag. The impressive little main buttress is split by two crack lines. I climbed them both, Dinsdale on the left in 1971, with Mick Myres and Spiney Norman, on the right in 1972 with Roger Gill. On the first I rested on a sling threaded round a large chockstone after becoming tired after attempting to clean the moss out of the overhanging crack above. The sling was not used to make upward progress, and the route was led on sight. A year later I climbed the steeper crack on the right. At twenty feet there was a peg in place, and obviously it had been attempted previously. I used the peg and a nut above to climb a difficult and overhanging wall. After hard free climbing I rejoined the crack where it widened and split another roof. Exhausted I plopped in four nuts, one almost on top of the other. They were totally unnecessary as the difficulties had now eased considerably; above the route was entirely free climbing. I recorded the route faithfully with six points of aid. To my mind I had made a reasonable attempt, for although clearly not fit enough to climb it free, I had not damaged the rock in any way, all the nuts being easily removed, and the peg had been placed previously by an unknown party. I could have gone back at least to do the climb without those four top nuts, knowing now what was to come, but I did not see much incentive, considering it to be cheating, somewhat, to return with pre-knowledge. (How one's ideals change.)

Although including the scrappy routes on the right-hand crag, Alan completely missed out of the guide my routes on the main buttress, not even acknowledging that it had been climbed. I thought it somewhat unjust. A famous Jackal came along, did the second ascent of both routes and, although he used the bottom two points of aid on the second route (Spiney Norman), he announced to the world that he had free-climbed them both. To add insult to injury, he renamed both climbs.

It was ironic that many people were informed of this 1976 'achievement' some five years after the first ascent and yet were unaware of the first ascent. Fortunately, Bob and Martin Berzins came along and completely free climbed the latter route, a fine piece of climbing, re-renaming it Spiney Norman. The climbs incidentally are now graded E2 and E3.

Alan Austin has had a remarkable climbing record. Not only has he produced very many brilliant climbs but he championed the need for free rock climbing. Amazingly, he married his climbing partner and managed during a tremendously active career to run a family business and raise three children. As an example of the extent of climbing, not only was he producing new and significant routes on Yorkshire gritstone and limestone and in the Lake District but he actually climbed every route in the Old Stanage guidebook. He has always been a fighter both in his climbing and also when defending his ethical code—no aid.

During the twenty years when Alan Austin was actively climbing and pioneering new routes, he saw a great deal of change. In fact, he was accountably responsible for the rapid swing away from aid climbing. "I would go to great lengths to get the right direction of the sport." Techniques and equipment also radically advanced. From the single hemp rope of Birkett's day, hawser-laid nylon was introduced, then purlon, which was even more supple, strong and durable. Climbs were done on doubled ropes which enabled running belays to be placed and used more easily. (Two ropes meant less friction and hence less drag.) Running belays improved beyond all conception, from no climbing protection at all, as in Birkett's era, first arrived the inserted chockstones of the 1950s (actually small pebbles that were jammed in cracks and then threaded with a sling) and then finally the artificial chockstones—nuts that were pre-threaded with a nylon sling.

Alan first saw nuts in the car-park at Langdale in 1961. These were actually the nuts of nut-and-bolt type that fasten cars together etc. They were simply drilled out and made smooth to get rid of the screw thread and then threaded with a nylon sling. The nut was jammed in a crack, and a snap-link karabiner enabled the climbing rope to run through the sling. At first Alan did not appreciate the true significance, and they were treated as something of a joke. Very rapidly their true potential dawned on the unsuspecting climbing world. Big, unprotected leads became a thing of the past, for one could use nuts without damaging the rock as a piton did. Nuts are now very sophisticated things: made from super-light and strong alloys, they vary in size upwards from fingernail size up to large hexagonal pieces of alloy not much less than a football.

Footwear too changed, from the cheap gym shoes or nailed boots of Birkett and Dolphin's day to the ultra-expensive and sophisticated close-fitting high-friction grip-rubber PA.

Climbing, when Alan Austin 'retired' in the mid 1970s, was a completely different game to that when Birkett, Peascod and Dolphin and their predecessors pioneered new routes. It has changed to such an extent that there can be no real comparison between climbing now and then. Before present-day climbers refer to their inflated standards, they should be able to solo Harlot Face E1 (Birkett, 1949) in nailed boots and Deer Bield Buttress E1 (Dolphin, 1951) in training shoes—the footwear they walked up to the crag in.

Austin remarked on this change, saying: "Before nuts arrived, you could always tell the hard climbers. They usually stood alone quietly in a corner of the bar and had a wild look in their eyes. Robin Smith was notable. When he spoke of routes, his piercing eyes seemed to expand with the excitement. They were great guys but you couldn't call them normal." Then with a smile, "Not like you and me."

Route name	Grade	Location	Comments
1956 Stickle Grooves	HVS	Pavey Ark, Langdale	
Eden Groove	HS	Deer Bield Crag, Langdale	
1957 Walthwaite Gully	MVS	Raven Crag, Walthwaite, Langdale	
Cascade	HVS	Pavey Ark	
1958 Peel Climb	MVS	Red Crag, Newlands	
The Hog's Back	VS	Gowder Crag, Borrowdale	

Route name	Grade	Location	Comments
By-Pass Route	HVS	Pavey Ark	
Stalag	VS	Pavey Ark	
Roundabout	VS	Pavey Ark	
Golden Slipper	HVS	Pavey Ark	
1959 Inertia	HVS	Gimmer Crag	
Troll's Corner	HVS	Pavey Ark	
1960 Rectangular Slab	VS	Pavey Ark	
Astra	E1	Pavey Ark	One point aid— now free; alt. with M. Metcalf
The Scabbard	VS	North Buttress, Bowfell	
Flat Crag Corner	VS	Flat Crags, Bowfell	
Red Groove	E1	Pavey Ark	
1961 Spec Crack	E1	Heron Crag, Eskdale	P. Walsh led
1962 Arcturus	HVS	Pavey Ark	
1963 Swastika	VS	Pavey Ark	
The Gibli	HVS	Bowfell	
Gimmer String	E1	Gimmer Crag	
Poacher	E1	Gimmer Crag	Alt. with M. Metcalf
Man of Straw	E1	White Ghyll	One peg aid— now free
Rough Ridge	VD	Side Pike	
1964 Bowfell Buttress			
Eliminate	HVS	Bowfell	
Gandalf's Groove	E1	Neckband Crag	
Sorbo	HVS	Blea Crag	
Bleabery Buttress	HVS	Blea Crag	
Brandy Wine	VS	Grey Buttress, Newlands	
1965 Rainmaker	E1	Pavey Ark	One peg aid— now free
Artefact	MVS	High Crag, Newlands	
Direct Route	VS	Grey Buttress, Newlands	
Angst	VS	Grey Buttress, Newlands	
Sheepbone Buttress	VD	Buttermere	
Carnival	E1	Eagle Crag, Buttermere	Var leads N. J. Soper and I. Roper
1966 Roundabout Direct	VS	Pavey Ark	
Chimney Variant	E2	White Ghyll	
Poker Face	E1	Pavey Ark	
Variation Traverse	HVS	White Ghyll	Alt. with Ken Wood
Razor Crack	E1	Neckband Crag	
Storm Groove	HVS	Hard Knott Crag	

Route name	Grade	Location	Comments
The Arete	MVS	Striddle Crag, Buttermere	
Jack's Route	MVS	Striddle Crag, Buttermere	
One Pitch	VS	Ling Crag	
The Purist	HVS	Ling Crag	
The Spur	HS	Green Crag	
The Crooked Man	HS	Buckstone Howe, Buttermere	
Numbskull	MVS	Green Crag	
Pedestal Corner	VS	Green Crag	
Paper Tiger	MVS	Green Crag	
1967 Grouter	S	Helm Crag, Langdale	
Warn Ghyll Buttress	MVS	Haystacks, Buttermere	
Carrion	HVS	Yew Crag	
Gemini	MVS	Haystacks	
Menshevick	HVS	Green Crag	
Saraband	HVS	Green Crag	
Cove Crack	VS	Yewdale Crag, Coniston	
1968 Gillette	E2	Neckband Crag	Ken Wood led
1969 Caravan Slab	MVS	Mart Crag, Coniston	
Boulder Buttress	VS	Mart Crag, Coniston	
1969 Diamond Buttress	VS	Mart Crag, Coniston	
Little Gem	VS	Mart Crag, Coniston	
The Heel	VS	Seathwaite Buttress	
Crescent Direct	VS	Pavey Ark	
Express Crack	HVS	Backbarrow Crag, Longsleddle	
1970 Brackenclock	E2	Pavey Ark	One peg + sling aid—now free
Little Corner	HVS	Pavey Ark	
1971 The Ragman's Trumpet	E2	Pavey Ark	Rod Valentine led
Haste Not Direct	E2	White Ghyll	
Flat Iron Wall	E1	Flat Crag, Bowfell	
1972 Whits End Direct	E1	Gimmer Crag	
'B' Buttress Variations	E1	Dow Crag	
1974 Efrafra	E2	Neckband Crag	Ed Grindley led
Hearth	HVS	Yew Crag, Buttermere	
1975 The Overhang Pitch	HVS	Dow Crag	

12

Pete Livesey
(12th September 1943–   )

In the early 1970s a number of harder routes began to emerge. Standards were slowly rising above that of the already very hard routes of Whillans, Brown, Crew, Smith, Austin and others. Often, though, the climbs were blighted by the use of a limited amount of artificial aid for progress or for resting. (Artificial aid takes the form of inserted 'nut' chockstones or, even worse, pegs which are then used as a handhold or a foothold.) Most of the hard route development was taking place in Wales, particularly with the 'discovery' of the Gogarth Sea Cliffs on the Isle of Anglesey. Lake District development, in both difficulty and quality, with the exception of but a handful of routes, was falling behind that in Wales.

Pete Livesey burst from obscurity with a series of routes that stung the entrenched climbing regime. His totally free ascent of the 'Great Buttress' on Goat Crag in Borrowdale, a route previously employing eight points of aid from both pitons and expansion bolts, produced a route that was much harder than the hardest Extreme route then climbed in Britain. This ascent matched any single advance in standard yet achieved in the entire history of rock climbing.

The route was named Footless Crow (E5 6b) because there was no place to land. Its combined difficulties, both mental and physical, are incredibly high and the climbing is so sustained that the 175-foot-long pitch keeps the climber hopping from one minute hold to the next.

Livesey's climbs left all gasping in his wake. At first there was disbelief and controversy, but his consistent performances showed that a whole 'brave new world' was possible. Rapidly climbers began realistically to examine his achievements and subsequently to mould themselves on his approach and techniques. Pete, then, was the 'superstar' who led a great renaissance in British free rock climbing. He generated a period of development that provided more high-quality hard routes than ever before, heralding what I regard as the true Golden Age of Lakeland climbing.

Pete began rock climbing later than most. In fact he was pioneering his major routes at an age when most rock climbers are thinking of hanging up their boots. His early days at school and college were spent running: he was a Junior International at middle-distance cross country.

Born in Huddersfield, next to a quarry incidentally, he first attended a local grammar school and then entered college with the intention of studying electrical engineering, but his dedication to his sport did not leave a great deal of time for study. Exam failures forced a decision: to continue his sport at a top level or become an electrical engineer. So at twenty years of age he dropped competitive running and took up caving and climbing, aiming to give himself more time to study! Soon weekends and evenings were spent pot-holing and occasionally climbing.

In 1965 it was again decision time as Pete became more and more interested in sport, particularly caving, where he had rapidly become one of Britain's top pot-holers. He decided he did not really want to become an engineer and went off to the West Indies for a year.

The attraction of the West Indies originated not from the sun-baked beaches but from information supplied by a Leeds University expedition of the previous year. It reported the existence of limestone caves large enough to swallow sizeable rivers, and it was in the exploration of the caves that Livesey's interest lay.

His early climbing included much work on gritstone, and he did his first Extreme when twenty-one years old: the overlapping wall in Llanberis Pass, North Wales. Shortly after this he took a big fall from the top of Joe Brown's very hard route Vector, on the Tremadoc cliffs. Luckily he escaped injury. Climbing only sporadically, by his own later standards he was not yet taking it seriously. Teacher training college followed the West Indies trip and resulted in work for the Mountain Association in both North Wales and the Lake District.

Steadily he was now beginning to climb more frequently, and in 1966 he put up his first new route, which lies on the very fine and grossly underrated Heron Crag in Eskdale. It took a bulging arete direct and pre-empted a route now known as Karma Sutra (VS) which traverses across the arete avoiding all the major difficulties. It was never recorded by the FRCC and was omitted from the guide, which is a great pity as the line is good, obviously Extreme and historically important.

Douk (HVS) in Yorkshire's great natural limestone amphitheatre marked the first of his progressively brilliant ascents on limestone. Later, in 1967, he made the second ascent of the Trolltyn Wall in Norway, with John Stanger. Fate seemed to be nudging Pete Livesey towards climbing, for he had not planned to be on the Troll Wall.

One of his breakthroughs in caving had been the first descent of the Mossdale Caverns, and he and his 'mates' had arranged to make the second descent. At the last minute Pete changed his schedule and opted for the Troll Wall. His six friends continued with the trip down the Mossdale Caverns. It rained hard and flooded the system: all six cavers were killed.

Canoeing became one of Livesey's major activities from this time through to 1970. As in running and caving, he excelled, becoming one of Britain's top white-water canoeists. The outbreak of foot and mouth disease in the winter of 1968 and the consequent restrictions on access to farmland ensured that his energies were again directed fully into climbing. First impressions are that climbing would be the most likely of Pete's interests to be restricted but the discovery (by Alan Austin) of a disused limestone quarry above Settle, directly accessible by road, provided the requisite facility.

Langcliffe Quarry suddenly had his full attention, and a number of very hard and bold climbs were accomplished. This was the turning-point for Pete, by 1970, had decided that climbing was the sport for him and that he was to give it his total dedication. He wrote:

Langcliffe can be said to be a fairly modern crag. Although modern equipment is virtually unusable on its protectionless lines, the mental strain associated with ascents of hard new routes is very much in evidence on the main crags. Technical standards are never high nor are the routes strenuous, but nearly all sustained and bold. The climbs on the three main sections, Main Wall, Central Wall and South Wall, are all on very clean rock, sometimes firm, sometimes suspect, one never really knows.

Until this time, although doing early ascents and a number of new routes, Pete had never really thought of himself as a climber. He had climbed mainly with members of the Phoenix Club from Huddersfield and described it as the kind of club where, "If you wanted to be in it you couldn't and if you didn't you were." After Langcliffe he realized that he had outstanding ability and learned the true meaning of his earlier ascents.

There followed a series of incredible routes on limestone, mainly free climbing the old aid routes. Pete said: "I had made a conscious decision to climb hard, the best routes on Limestone were generally peg routes and I climbed these free. My ambition was to climb harder than anyone else and pioneer harder routes than anything yet achieved."

Philosophies that Livesey had previously applied to athletics, canoeing and pot-holing now dictated his approach to climbing. He combined his determination to be the best with physical fitness and an intense programme of training. Devising a hard traverse on a climbing wall at Scunthorpe (a climbing wall is purpose built to enable climbing indoors and so allows climbing whatever the weather or conditions), he completed it, without resting, twenty times each evening. Pete said: "Training on the wall made an incredible difference. It really got my standards going."

Pete entered the climbing scene with an outlook different from that of the then current activists. The routes he pioneered were a new conception of difficulty, and they shook the establishment. Consequently many of these early ascents, particularly on lime-stone, were shrouded in controversy.

His* totally free ascent of Face Route at Goredale Scar, in Yorkshire, was the scene of an early controversy. Once a route climbed totally by aid from pegs, it now became a focal point of the new ethical movement. Unknown to Livesey the route had been climbed a few days prior to his ascent with three points of aid. This considerable achievement had been carried out by two top climbers, Ken Wood and Alan Austin. Consequently when Pete, an unknown climber, climbed it totally free, with J. Sheard, he was disbelieved—how could anyone climb so hard? This, coupled with the fact that it was rumoured that Sheard had been seen climbing with slings for aid, brought about massive con-demnation of the team by the climbing establishment. The Yorkshire Mountaineering Club were so incensed with Pete's alleged break of ethics that they refused to put any of his routes in the forthcoming limestone guide.

What people did not realize at the time was that Pete could not be judged by existing performances, that his ability belonged to the next generation, to the super fit, extremely talented and enlightened generation that was to dominate the mid and late 1970s. Pete Livesey was not just another climber—he was a rock athlete.

Subsequent performances vindicated Pete, and his routes are now amongst the best in the Yorkshire guide. What did become apparent was that he had top-roped Face Route prior to the ascent, and this he openly admitted. His approach to new routing, and a significant factor in the extreme difficulty of these routes, was the way he prepared a route. He no longer top-roped routes as this was generally considered unethical but began to abseil down the lines primarily to clean them (that is to 'garden off' the vegetation, to remove loose rocks and spikes and to clean off the moss with a wire brush) but also to inspect the route closely. Modern equipment in the form of abseiling devices (the figure of eight Descender etc) and 'Jumars' or 'cloggers' make going up and down a route on a rope fixed from above a simple activity.

This approach to new routing was not really new—after all,

Herford and Sansom pre-inspected the Great Flake on Central Buttress a number of times—but it was now a whole lot more sophisticated. It became known as 'the professional approach' and of course was to produce some superb and clean climbs.

Rock climbing with its ultra-sophisticated equipment and techniques was being dragged up to a technical level commensurate with these innovations. It became, however, a sport completely different to that of rock climbing a generation earlier.

Livesey's early Yorkshire limestone routes were also climbed in a spirit of increasing competition. This helped further to push up climbing standards. Pete wrote *Arms Like A Fly* in 1972, telling of his and Sheard's first free ascent of Central Wall on Kilnsey Crag: "The pace was hotting up in Yorkshire now, we'd had it virtually to ourselves for six months, now there were two teams scrapping for Kilnsey's prize. We'd snatched Diedre the week before, lifted it from the same team that were ahead of us in the Central Wall stakes."

He continued with an account of the climb which gives an insight into modern Extreme climbing: "Neither of us said much—I was now engrossed in fright. The start is a vicious little pull over a roof to gain a ramp rising leftwards. Ten feet of climbing and you're committed, but so far the holds were good and I was finding lots of little threads below the guardian overlap I was following. I felt very unhappy up there, I'd used a lot of energy getting over the initial bulge and things were going to get a lot steeper in the next hundred feet."

It also shows something of the modern climbing ethic: "The problem was to get my left hand on the hold and make a huge swing right for a flake, but the move was perfectly protected. I kept thinking—if I fall on the peg, will it be aid?"

It was in 1971 that Pete first applied his new philosophy and techniques to the Lake District, with Sally Free and Easy (E2 5b5c with one point of aid on top pitch), climbing the big wall of Crescent Buttress and then following a corner groove to the top. Again there was a flare-up with Alan Austin. The latter, this time climbing with the powerful Rod Valentine, claimed they had ascended the wall prior to Pete's ascent, albeit only starting half way up the pitch from the gully and not finishing up the corner but merely scrambling up vegetated ground. Again Pete was threatened that his route would not go into the forthcoming guidebook (being prepared jointly by Austin and Valentine for the FRCC).

I think it was a genuine mistake by Austin, for Pete had climbed the wall sometime previously—with the inscrutable Barry Rogers. They climbed the wall one evening, when they were both working at an outdoor pursuits centre at Humphry Head. After the first hard long pitch, darkness fell and Pete intended to return. Barry on the other hand was not so keen! Barry said to me that Pete kept leaving him messages with the centre's receptionist: "Barry, it's on for tonight," and the next fine evening, "Let's go tonight, Barry," and after a few weeks of Barry carefully avoiding Pete, "Barry this is your last chance—Pete." This was the signal for Barry to come out of hiding!

Pete, frustrated, climbed the top pitch solo with a back rope and using one point of aid (climbed free by John Adams and Pete Botterill sometime later). His ascent of the top pitch came after Austin's ascent of the bottom wall and this, I am sure, is why Austin thought that their route 'Ragman's Trumpet' was a first ascent. Controversy apart, Sally Free and Easy is an infinitely better route than 'Ragman's Trumpet', and in the end this is the only thing that matters.

A year later Pete ascended Fine Time (E3 6a) on Raven Crag, Langdale, which utilized a long sling for aid on an old, *in-situ* peg (climbed free by Pete Botterill and Jeff Lamb). The route, apart from one point of aid, free-climbed an old peg route called Kaisergebirge Wall and was superb and very hard—a fine achievement in fact. Again there was boring controversy, but now people were beginning to see through the smokescreens laid by others, and the climate of Lakeland climbing was taking on a new dynamism.

In 1973 Pete took a long trip to the States, his second, where he learned an awful lot about techniques and where his eyes were opened to the possibilities. He knew now "what was possible and what was not". Notable ascents, such as the third ascent of Direct North Buttress and the second ascent of L'Esqualer, a hard 5.11 lay back, and a host of other routes on the steep granite faces of the Yosemite Valley honed the Livesey 'machine' to peak performance.

The following year, 1974, was a big year for Pete Livesey and one of Lakeland climbing's greatest. His routes were monsters, Eastern Hammer, (E3 6a), Dry Gasp (E4 6a), Nagasaki Grooves

(E4 6b) and Footless Crow (E5 6b). All followed and free-climbed the lines of existing aid routes. Probably the best, and possibly the easiest, of this incredible bunch of routes, Bitter Oasis, was however a self-conceived line. Pete explained the origin of the name to me: "Virtually led on sight, I climbed the very steep groove all the time making for an apparent glacis. On arrival the oasis turned out to be an overlapping and vertical wall and the climbing remained very hard with nowhere to rest. I was forced to continue up the steep rock above to a belay ledge some thirty feet higher."

It is hard not to eulogize about this route for it is truly magnificent, one of Lakeland's finest modern routes in fact. The climbing, though not at maximum desperation, is very hard for every move of its full 165-foot length. It is not particularly the situation that impresses one, although there is much 'raw space' about, for Goat Crag is not the most beautiful of crags, but it is the totally absorbing and intricate nature of the climbing. Each move must be thought about and executed only with difficulty; the intensity and commitment of the climbing provide the beauty.

It is prudent to examine the method of grading Extreme climbs at this stage to put Livesey's routes into context.

In the fifties there existed Extreme climbs (E1). Joe Brown and friends extended this to a two-tier system, Extremely Severe and Exceptionally Severe. This was extended again to three tiers in the late sixties, devised in the Lakes by John Adams and Colin Read: now there were Mild Extremes, Extremes and Hard Extremes. To cater for the new generation of Extreme climbs originated by Pete, an open-ended system, starting at E1 and extending to E5, for Footless Crow, was devised, again in the Lake District. This was supplemented by the purely technical grading from 5a to 6b for Extreme climbs. This outwardly complicated system of dual grading has been found necessary for today's highly technological and physiological climbing world, for now a climb may be extremely technical and/or serious.

A technical climb is one that is physically and mentally difficult to execute. Physical difficulty in climbing presents itself in numerous forms. The climb may be strenuous, involving, say, hand jamming up a wide-ish overhanging crack or finger-locking/semi-laybacking up a thin crack. (Laybacking is a technique where the climber bends at the waist and places his/her feet near the hands, pushes with the legs and pulls with the arms; the opposite action locks the climber into position. Try it on a door frame if you wish—it is not easy! Finger-locking consists of placing the fingers in a thin crack, twisting them until they jam and then pulling up on them.) Or the climb may be precarious, where brute strength is not applicable as on a slab using only minute rugosities where it is the balance and neat footwork of the climber that keeps him *in situ*.

When there is a sequence of hard physical moves, or the way up is complicated and involves different types of climbing, then this sort of climb is regarded as 'technical'. The hardest technical climb would be given 6b or even 6c (note: a technical grade is given to each individual pitch) and would be graded E3 if it were not for another very important factor—seriousness.

Seriousness is decided by what would happen to the climber if he fell off. All Birkett's and Peascod's routes and the routes of pioneers leading up to their era were extremely serious— irrespective of technical grading—simply because, if they had fallen off, they would have most probably been killed. Today, however, with modern protection techniques, nut runners etc, if the climber falls off, he will most probably not be killed. On some extremely technical/hard climbs where there is no possibility of placing protection (note: in the Lake District the use of piton protection is frowned upon and bolt runners are ethical suicide), the hardest of these climbs is given E5. It is this constant factor of seriousness that separates climbing from all other physically difficult sports.

During the summer of 1974 Pete raised the level of climbing from 'steady' E3 to stupendous E5. Of course Footless Crow was the hardest route but both Nagasaki Grooves and Dry Gasp weighed in at E4. Amazingly (and it is very easy to run out of superlatives when describing Livesey's summer of 1974), he soloed these latter two routes in a single day. On different Borrowdale crags, Great End and Upper Falcon Crag, they were a grade harder than anything climbed by anybody else.

One could logically assume that this more than impressive achievement was the result of much planning and preparation, but not so. Pete, after hanging around Keswick all day Saturday waiting for his mates to show, decided not to waste Sunday! He first climbed Nagasaki Grooves free, a Colin Read and John

Adams route on which they had employed an unfortunate amount of aid, using only a back-rope for protection. Pointed to the line by Ray McHaffie, the irrepressible Guru of Borrowdale, he was mischievously informed that the route had never been climbed— the aim being to beguile Pete into the 'tender trap' of over-aiding.

Passing that little test, he moved on to Upper Falcon Crag and produced the aptly named Dry Gasp. Soloing the first pitch, he then back roped the main top pitch. His method of back roping consisted of making up six-foot loops in the rope and securing them to his harness, fixing the end of the rope to a belay and then climbing. After six feet of climbing he released a loop of rope enabling him to climb another six feet, i.e. twelve feet in all. He placed nut runners as he climbed, so protecting himself.

On Nagasaki Grooves the system worked OK, for he fell from the move into the bottom of the groove, below the crux, with no serious consequences, but here he had fastened the separate loops of the rope to his harness by means of individual karabiners. For Dry Gasp, possibly to save weight, he fastened the loops directly into the single-harness karabiner. Before, it had been relatively simple to whip a hand off, unclip the krab and drop the loop. On Dry Gasp, however, to detach the loop from the single karabiner became very awkward. The climbing is thin and sustained, and it is difficult to let go of the rock at all, let alone fiddle with extracting a rope from a reluctant karabiner.

Pete found himself being pushed to stretch the rope against the pull of the belay. It produced a sticky feeling in the throat and hence the name of the route! To find this level of commitment is not easy but when I asked Pete how, he gave a very simple answer: "I knew I could do them."

The biggest breakthrough of course was Footless Crow (E5 6b), and this, combined with the Right Wall (E5 6a) on the Dinnas Cromlech in Wales, added up to one heck of a summer's climbing for Pete.

There are many legends attached to these ascents, the most popular being that Pete abseiled down and practised the routes for weeks prior to his ascent. These tales are, of course, wildly exaggerated. In the case of Footless Crow the programme was that he spent an afternoon cleaning the route from abseil (i.e. removing the moss and lichen with a wire brush) and returned with Jack Hammond to attempt the climb but failed on the first hard moves. This was followed by more jumaring and inspection. Returning again to attempt the route, it remained very wet after rain, so he again examined the crux from a rope. On the next visit the route was climbed.

An interesting twist of irony was that Bill Freelands and Ray McHaffie were at the crag and watched the ascent—ironic because it was Bill Freelands who had first ascended the route with expansion bolts and pitons for aid. Apparently Bill, a good climber with a number of first ascents to his credit, could not believe his own eyes. So impressed was he with Pete's ascent that he gave up climbing! Ray too was deeply impressed with the Pete Livesey style of climbing. He described it as very smooth and almost effortless, as though Pete were climbing a Very Difficult climb (VD) not the hardest route in the country.

Pete's last route in the Lakes was climbed with Pete Gomersall on Raven Crag, Thirlmere, in 1978. It is very hard indeed, has not yet had a complete second ascent and is graded E5 6b. The years between that great year of 1974 and this route 'Das Kapital' were filled with his very hard, but more importantly high-quality, routes. His influence not only on Lakeland but on British climbing has been profound, for Livesey's routes are stretched around Britain, on many different types of cliffs and on many different types of rock. Be it gritstone, limestone, slate, rhyolite, granite or quartzite, from the Lake District through Derbyshire, Yorkshire and Wales to Land's End, Pete can boast a string of top-quality climbs. His insatiable appetite for rock does not end in Britain for he has climbed extensively in the 'rock' Alps and elsewhere in Europe.

He was climbing in places like the immaculate two-thousand-foot limestone Verdon Gorge in southern France when other British rock climbers were idling away their time in the storm-ridden Alps, unable to climb because of poor conditions but totally unaware of any alternative. His guidebook to French rock climbing, although not perhaps as accurate as some would like, has been a tremendous enlightenment to the British rock-climbing public. Many climbers now prefer this area to the tourist-laden Yosemite Valley. There is no doubt that Pete has been one of our most innovative climbers.

Unusually perhaps, but most certainly in the current trend amongst top rock climbers, Pete has no ambitions in the big mountains. He is not interested in the 'snow bashing' type of climbing associated with expedition mountaineering such as that performed by Chris Bonnington and Reinhold Messner. Perhaps this can be explained when one realizes the extremely specialist nature of rock climbing and the considerable degree of dedication now required to climb the top Extreme standard.

Do not, however, believe that Pete does not love the natural beauty of the British mountains, particularly the Lakeland Fells, for he is not merely a chalk-covered athlete (chalk is light magnesium carbonate in which the climber dips his hands to improve his grip before making a hard move—it originated from the hot and sweaty Yosemite Valley in the USA), blinded to his sport: he is a rock climber with all that that implies. Pete wrote in his article 'Lakeland Commentary':

> But the hills are different, try the slate quarried slopes of Coniston; escape from the winds behind the lowest of slaty huts, to be surprised by the warm, black jingling caverns of the slate miner fitted in exquisite compaction between the earliest of Lakeland highways, the salt men's Walna Scar Road, and the death-hollowed perfection of Blind Tarn. . . . Nor is it the myriad interlocking of visual shows confined only to three dimensions; time packs more. There are times to be in the Lakes—on a winter morn with the black, glass-smooth, ice-hard lake sinking into bright hoary mountains; in the autumn sun, whose heat is trebled by the warmth of a copper-coloured land sandwiched between lakes and a sky that has to be blue.

Winter climbing, that is climbing on snow and ice, is another aspect of the sport that Pete professes to have little interest in. Admitting that he had done a little winter climbing, he assured me that he preferred skiing in winter. I, however, have other information, for chatting one winter evening to Jill Lawrence (a one-time regular climbing companion to Pete who has accompanied him on a number of new routes) in the Clachaig Bar in Glencoe, she informed me that his rare winter climbing included a stroll up Raven's Gully, Grade V, on the Buachaille Etive Mor—one of Scotland's hardest winter routes.

In this highly technological age of ultra-sophisticated nut runners, 'friends' (a camming device which, by pulling a bar, enables the spring-loaded cams first to contract and then to expand to the exact width of a crack. They will even hold a fall when inserted upside-down in an expanding roof crack), ultrathin nylon slings and light alloy karabiners, one can easily be fooled into thinking that present-day climbers are not of equal 'mettle' to their predecessors. It is certainly a different sport now to that of only a generation previously but not really all that different. To reiterate Jim Birkett's words: "Botterill, Herford, Sansom—that type has always been there and is still with us today, but I will say in Botterill's day they didn't know what was possible, today they do. There will always be real climbers though. Every sport has its naturals—with application and dedication they become superstars."

Pete Livesey has most certainly proved this with his breathtaking soloing exploits (soloing is to climb alone, without a rope or any other form of protection from falling; soloing with a backrope is to use self-belaying protection techniques). Possibly his finest soloing achievement was an early ascent of 'Lord of the Rings' (E2), a twelve-hundred-foot traverse of the East Buttress of Scafell. This very hard route was first climbed in 1969 by Colin Read and John Adams. They took two days to complete the ascent, and it was a marvellous pioneering effort. Such was the magnitude of the climb that it waited a further six years for a second ascent. Ed Cleasby and myself made this second ascent one fine early May day—the earliest opportunity in 1975. Within a week, the spell broken, it had another two ascents.

When Pete Livesey came along to make, most probably, the fifth ascent, he found two parties ahead of him on the route. After back roping the initial crux pitch, he went on to solo past the other two roped parties—so accomplishing the fifth ascent! The route is long, exposed and difficult. It was a typical Livesey achievement—audacious yet admirable.

Pete says that his ambition for the future is to keep with climbing and enjoy it, that although there may be lines climbed now that are harder than his hardest achievements, he considers a long, sustained route much more personally satisfying than a 'line' with a single isolated desperate move (6c or above). Pete recently again proved his athletic diversity and excellence by winning what he calls the "British Super Looney Championship", in reality an event involving top athletes from a number of fields and entitled 'Survival of the Fittest'. I should think Pete knows a thing or two about survival by now.

Throughout the 1970s Pete Livesey motivated a huge force of

fit and dedicated climbers. His ideals brought about an abundance of good and super-hard routes, at a time when others were oblivious to the possibilities. But that is the hallmark of a great pioneer, is it not?

	Route name	Grade	Location	Comments
1971	Sally Free & Easy	E2 5a 5c	Pavey Ark	One point aid
1972	Fine Time	E3 6a	Raven Crag, Langdale	One point aid
1973	Raindrop	E1	Black Crag	
1974	Footless Crow	E5 6a	Goat Crag	
	Bitter Oasis	E3 6a 6a	Goat Crag	
	Eastern Hammer	E3 6a	Gimmer Crag	
	Day Gasp	E4 6a	Upper Falcon Crag	Same day
	Nagasaki Grooves	E4 6b(ffa)	Great End	soloed
1975	Bowfell Buttress			
	Eliminate	E1 5b	Bowfell	Solo
	Rough	E2 5c	Dow Crag	
	Tumble	E3 6a	Dow Crag	
1976	Breaking Point	E2 5c 5c		
		5c	Gimmer Crag	
	Lost Colonies	E3 5c	High Crag	
	Lost Horizons	E4 6a 5c	East Buttress, Scafell	One point aid
1977	Gabriel	E1 5b	Castle Rock	
	Peels of Laughter	E4 6b	Raven Crag, Thirlmere	
	Tristar	E4 5b 6a	Black Crag	
1978	Hiroshima	E4 6a	Great End	
	Das Kapital	E5 6b 6b	Raven Crag, Thirlmere	

Index